Summer *by* the Sea

Summer *by* the Sea

Cottages from Watch Hill to Little Compton

THOMAS A. KLIGERMAN

PHOTOGRAPHS BY READ McKENDREE

Summer *by* the Sea

Cottages—the simple, unpretentious kind that dot Rhode Island's ocean shore—are never just houses. Sixty summers spent along the coast, in a place resonating with memories and decades-long friendships, have taught me this now-obvious lesson. I was raised in a family who spent the warm months in the southwest corner of the nation's smallest state, renters in tiny Weekapaug, a borough of the larger town of Westerly, which anchors the beach communities along Block Island Sound. Over the years, we moved from an 1880s shingled cottage to another house, barely a hundred yards away, built in the 1920s by our new landlord's father. We spent two years in the first, more in the second, and although the first was a small Victorian and the second a diminutive farmhouse, they were linked by their shingled walls, gently burnished interiors, and gaggles of worn wicker furniture. The combination of weathering wood, ocean air, and memory imbues houses like these with a quiet, unmistakable soul.

I am now a Weekapaug resident in a shingled house I designed as an architectural madeleine to be shared with my family. This book is a personal ode as much as an architectural history or tour of the southern edge of the state. As an architect, I will tell a Rhode Island tale through the lens of sixteen houses that capture, for me, the essence of summer. The story features the work of renowned architects, living and long gone. Unknown architects, their names squirreled away in building department archives, designed a few. And we may never know who built the others. Perhaps a farmer or long-forgotten ancestor took up hammer, nails, and lumber, relying on local tradition and common sense to create what has become a summer sanctuary within sight of the water or close enough to benefit from the Atlantic's coastal climate.

The houses range in size and form, but they are related in material and detail—cousins rather than siblings. They are manageable in size, thin on today's luxuries but linked by satisfying what one needs, not necessarily all of what one wants. Grayed cedar shingles sheath the exteriors; paint, in a range of colors, trims windows, shutters, and doors. Inside, the houses are lined with wood: pine, fir, or occasionally cypress. Older buildings lack paneling and insulation—nails holding the shingles poke through the wall boards—a not-so-minor hazard. Floors glow with the patina of summers of footsteps. All has mellowed—ceilings, doors, moldings, old arts and crafts or secondhand furniture. An unpretentious, welcoming character evokes memories through the aroma of wood, the salty wash of the ocean breezes, and the creak of wooden stairs.

Unique histories—intangibles rather than wood, stone, and glass—differentiate one house from the next. One feels the palpable presence of the owners who came before. These intangibles can be memories, stories of grandparents, cousins, parents—even strangers or local lore. Restorations, renovations, and how previous inhabitants tinkered with the cottages are rungs in a house's evolution, defining marks left by each succeeding familial wave. Design choices might have been guided by a longing for connection—to the land, to a view, or to another building from an owner's past in an altogether different location. But all these layers bring to life an ever-evolving dream about what life on the shore should be.

Our journey moves along the northeast arc of Rhode Island's coast from Westerly and the Pawcatuck River at Connecticut, across Narragansett Bay and the Sakonnet River to Little Compton hard up against Massachusetts. As the seagull flies, the trip is a mere thirty-seven miles. But the combination of history, geography, and architecture captures summers redolent of a sail in a wooden catboat, lying in the dunes on July Fourth, clambakes, rose hip jam, and rainy nights around a jigsaw puzzle spread across an old card table.

Along the Coast

The road toward the Rhode Island coast twists and narrows—six lanes to four, then four to two. The drive takes me through brush-like woods, acres of slender, gray-barked trees, and saplings, mere feet apart. Gone are many of the massive oak trees, vertiginous sugar maples, and giant beeches of the ancient forest. Those trees were cleared centuries ago, first by native peoples who needed to plant for sustenance and later by English settlers further domesticating the land. In the early twentieth century, as farming moved west, the woodlands of the time before native tribes and colonials began to reestablish. Running through the woods are miles of pale green and yellow lichen-covered stone walls.

Thousands of years ago, receding glaciers left behind a mix of sand, clay, and those stones. Farmers breaking the land or tilling fields brought these rocks to the surface, each one requiring a stop to excavate. Many were wrestled into foundations for houses, but most were stacked to create walls bordering fields, containing livestock and defining property lines. These stony boundaries are a beloved feature of New England's landscape from Canada south to the Atlantic—a sprawling stone calligraphy, rising and falling with centuries of frost heaves and spring thaws.

The sky brightens as the land flattens to reveal the Atlantic's horizon, a slash of cobalt blue or mournful gray, depending on the weather. I am in the southwest corner of Rhode Island, near the Connecticut line, a network of inlets and coves bound in a drift of marshes, dunes, and barrier islands. A string of saltwater ponds, among them Winnapaug, Quonochontaug, Ninigret, and Trustom, stretches along the coast. Separated from the ocean by dunegrass-covered beaches, these low-lying areas stretch between the hills and stony headlands at Watch Hill eastward to the mouth of Narragansett Bay, New England's largest estuary. Glaciers carved undulating valleys into hard stones like granite, and when the earth warmed, those areas filled with sea water creating 150 square miles of water and 400 miles of shoreline. Islands divide Narragansett Bay into the Eastern and Western Passages, watery highways for an array of tankers, freighters, fishing trawlers, and silent fleets of sailing dinghies, schooners, and America's Cup-class sloops. With its shoulder against the eastern side of the bay, Little

A Beetle Cat, a mainstay of New England sailing, moored at the Weekapaug Yacht Club.

Compton's fields and farmland blend into the nook of Massachusetts and Cape Cod beyond.

Rhode Island's coast is in constant flux, alive with change. Summer tides and wind work away at the shoreline—anything near the water is fair game. Wild cards are the major storms that slam into the New England coast, altering the topography and geology in sometimes shocking ways. The ocean becomes a massive fire hose destroying everything in its path—mostly bludgeon, sometimes scalpel. Hurricane Irene and Superstorm Sandy cut channels from the ocean into the saltwater ponds burying communities like Misquamicut yards deep in sand. But these storms pale compared to the Great September Gale of 1815, which inundated towns along Narragansett Bay, dropping ships onto Providence's streets, and scrubbing all the trees off Napatree Point in Watch Hill. The Great New England Hurricane of 1938 breached barrier beaches, altering the shape and hydrology of the peaceful ponds. A high-water mark on a brick building in the port of Wickford indicates the crest of the storm surge and hints at the mash of boats and splintered docks that jammed the streets amid ruined buildings. The storm destroyed houses and iconic buildings like the 1899 Weekapaug Inn, left in a pile of shattered timber and broken glass. Houses were tossed inland, tumbling over dune and pond. Miraculously, some landed nearly intact, and they were eventually lifted onto new foundations.

The coast is a remarkably resilient web of native grasses, shrubs, and trees anchoring the earth. Laurels, multi-trunk shadblow, chokecherries, and oaks populate the land, each with its distinctive color and habit. Non-natives like privet, blue hydrangea, rosa rugosa, and Queen Anne's lace, all introduced from overseas, are part of the green tapestry. These plants ensure an extraordinarily rich variety of wildlife—squirrels, foxes, opossum, weasels, bobcats, and rabbits. The waterways are nurseries for striped bass, bluefish, mackerel, and menhaden. The sandy flats and jumbled rocky areas provide habitat for quahogs, soft-shell clams, crabs, lobster, limpets, and snails. There are almost too many bird species to mention: sandpipers, doves, goldfinches, wrens, cardinals, red-tailed hawks, and bald eagles. Ospreys tumble into the ocean to emerge with struggling silver fish. Less in evidence are the quiet garter snakes and diamondback terrapins thriving in the woods and wetlands. Thin is the line between us and nature.

Sounds, like the scents of salty air and the musk of low tide, are integral to the coast. The hoot of owls, a chorus of spring peepers, and the eerie nighttime howl of coyotes join the rhythm of waves on the beach—these are the melodies of the shore. Likewise, the staccato of the Native American words adds to the music of the state. These tribal names ring with local rhythm: Matunuck, Aquidneck, Sakonnet, Narrangansett, and Misquamicut. Translations are rooted in the land and wildlife—High Observation Place, Black Goose Abode, Rocky Outlet, People of the Small Point, Red Salmon. All speak to the land and its abundance. I love these names and the way they conjure the natural setting.

Wampanoag, Narragansett, Pequot, and other tribal societies were sophisticated and complex. Among the most powerful Indigenous groups in

CLOCKWISE FROM UPPER LEFT: Houses along the beach in Misquamicut, c. 1890. Hurricane damage, 1938. J. A. Williams, Bliss Farm, Portsmouth, c. 1875. Block Island stone walls, c. 1880.

Watch Hill Harbor, c. 1890.

Southeast Lighthouse, Mohegan Bluffs, Block Island, c. 1875.

Isaac Bell house, McKim, Mead & White, Newport, 1883.
William Watts Sherman house, H. H. Richardson, Newport, 1876.

New England, they inhabited villages along the coast, using the rich natural resources and access to the ocean for sustenance and trade. The fertile plains supported the cultivation of maize, beans, and squash. They fished, hunted deer, rabbit, and other animals that shared the meadows, forests, and shoreline. They lived in harmony with nature in seasonal villages of wigwams, shelters made of bent saplings covered with tree bark.

The early seventeenth century saw the arrival of the Europeans, who settled along the coast, bringing change to the Narragansett and other Indigenous tribes. The initial interactions with the native people were based on tentative trust and trade. The settlers relied on the locals for guidance to cultivate the land and survive the demanding environment. The Narragansett traded animal pelts, wampum, and food; the Europeans provided metal goods like guns and tools, as well as textiles and trinkets like glass beads, mirrors, and bells. Cooperation was soon overshadowed as the settlers encroached more and more on native lands. The Narragansett were drawn into colonial conflicts like the 1636–38 Pequot War and King Philip's War of 1675–76, a conflict that devastated the native tribes. By the late seventeenth century, the Narragansett had been displaced from much of their ancestral territory, their numbers and societies dwindling through assimilation or enslavement. In the ensuing years, the land became predominantly agricultural, largely livestock, sheep at first and then cattle as culinary tastes changed. Dairy farms continue to flourish, as is evident in the creameries throughout the state.

Roger Williams founded the Colony of Rhode Island and Providence Plantations in 1636 as a place of religious freedom and tolerance, with a wary but respectful acceptance of the native peoples. The Colony was feisty from the get-go, the first to declare independence, on May 4, 1776. It was the only one of the original New England colonies not founded as a religious settlement. Two significant buildings, the 1763 Truro Synagogue, the earliest in the country, and the 1699 Quaker Great Friends Meeting House, are testaments to the view that all religions were welcome.

Rhode Island's architecture has a traceable, distinctly American lineage, different from the architecture brought here by European settlement. Our country is brimming with examples of borrowed architecture: Georgian houses, Norman and Loire Valley copies, Greek Revival churches, Gothic college campuses, and Mediterranean train stations like the one in downtown Westerly. Immigrants brought their culture and historical building styles from their homelands. And others have built aspirational buildings hoping to project a new identity linked to important established foreign styles. But I am drawn to a nearly unfettered American architecture, one that developed here in Rhode Island: the shingle style.

Originally this approach was known as the "free classical" or "modern colonial" style. "Shingle style" would have to wait roughly seventy years until it was adopted by architectural historian Vincent Scully, who coined the term in his 1955 book *The Shingle Style: Architectural Theory and Design from Richardson to the Origins of Wright*. In simplest terms, the shingle style is a blend of Victorian stick style architecture and early American colonial houses brought together to form a distinctly homegrown architecture.

Newport Casino, McKim, Mead & White, Newport, 1879.

Imagine, as a starting point, colonial houses in Massachusetts like Nantucket's shingled 1686 Jethro Coffin house or the clapboard 1734 Ashley House in Deerfield. Their forms are rudimentary: a simple roof is folded with low eaves front and back meeting in a single ridge. A protruding brick chimney gathers the smoke from a cluster of fireplaces at the center of the building. From time to time, simple, box-like extensions provide additional needed space: a shed attached to the side or a protruding gabled form. The iconic version is the cat slide the continuation of the roof down the back, giving the house the classic New England asymmetrical silhouette known as a saltbox, named for colonial-era storage containers. The elemental geometric form of these houses reflects their straightforward floor plans.

Now picture the filigree of painted columns, beams, cross bracing, window moldings, and door casings of a Victorian house. These decorative flourishes embellish buildings ranging from a simple Gothic-style cottage to a large complex composition of turrets, window bays, balconies, and importantly, porches. Tall spindly brick chimneys sprout from the roof. These houses vary greatly in expressive and singular ways. They are far more expansive than the colonial houses: floor plans express the various shaped rooms within the building—octagonal dining rooms, circular parlors within towers capped with chocolate pot domes, and a panoply of porches.

Enclosing them are geometries of diagonals and stick-like decoration that contrast with the nearly unadorned box of the colonial house.

Blend the two houses and you have the shingle style. Hidden beneath the taut skin of cedar shingles, the structure is no longer evident the way it was in the stick style. The house becomes asymmetrical, porches and balconies are added, as well as scooped-out second-floor loggias. The building reaches out into the landscape—porches, open or screened, capture sunlight and breezes. There is a stronger emphasis of the horizontal, of reacting to the specifics of a site and melding into the land. Often the chimneys become squatter than their Victorian predecessors.

And the plans are something new altogether. They encompass the Victorian variety of shapes, but the rooms tend to blend more, one into the next. These open plans are modern compared with preceding centuries of discrete rooms. Although there are specific rooms for certain functions, the hall, a sort of combination living room and foyer, spills into other rooms, separated in many cases by open archways. Stairs pour down into this space, which opens through tall windows to the porches and landscape.

Vincent Scully identifies the William Watts Sherman house as the first example of the style. Designed in 1876 by Henry Hobson Richardson, the building was asymmetrical with organizing horizontal elements and only partially shingled. It still includes Victorian stick style cross bracing and structural expression. Working in Richardson's office at that time was a young architect named Stanford White, who was entrusted with designing an elaborate library and staircase addition. White later joined fellow Richardson employee Charles Follen McKim and colleague William Rutherford Mead to form McKim, Mead & White Architects.

In 1879 *New York Herald* publisher James Gordon Bennett Jr. gave the new firm its first major commission, the Newport Casino. The building, on fashionable Bellevue Avenue, opened in the summer of 1879, putting McKim, Mead & White on the map. Within a year they were designing other important shingle style houses for Samuel Tilton, Frances L. Skinner, and perhaps most famously, cotton broker Isaac Bell. The new style caught on. One need only look at the work of English-born Ernest Coxhead or New York transplant Bernard Maybeck in San Francisco to see how rapidly the style spread across the country. Architects John Calvin Stevens in Maine, William Ralph Emerson and Robert Swain Peabody in Boston, and Charles L. Bevins in Jamestown produced extraordinary shingle style examples. Bruce Price had a very personal version in his early designs for Tuxedo Park, New York.

The houses were modern for their time, very simple elemental forms sheathed in cedar. Many were embellished with colonial influences: classical pediments, turned spindles and stair balusters, fluted colonnettes, and dentilated entablatures, though these were often at a diminutive scale, playing second fiddle to the expanses of cedar. An iconic example of the simplicity of this new style was the William G. Low house in Bristol, Rhode Island, designed by McKim, Mead & White in 1887. The cottage is one grand gesture, the simplest of gabled forms. No additions or extraneous elements temper the big idea. There is a porch, but it's carved into the shingled volume, not tacked on. Buildings like the Low house continue to be studied and reinterpreted by contemporary architects. They rise along the length of Rhode Island's coast, sprinkled in the landscape, wrapped in cedar shingles.

It is the spirit of the older houses that this book aims to document, discuss, and admire. The houses that I have selected are not necessarily the largest or most elaborate. These houses address the spirit of summer on the Rhode Island coast as much as the style itself. Each has its own personality expressed through wood, nails, paint, and glass. The very wealthy built elaborate mansions along the Rhode Island coast, but the small houses in this book have a character that reflects my memories of life along the shore. They are far from mansions. They exhibit simplicity and materiality—visible studs, joists, rafters, and planking, cottages waiting for their estival moment in the sun. Walking across a porch or through the rooms is like beating a drum. The interiors carry the scent of years of cozy fires and mellowed wood.

My journey along the coast from Watch Hill to Little Compton will focus on cottages and houses in Newport County as well as in Washington County, which is known in these parts as "South County." We will visit eight coastal towns and sixteen houses that unite in a Rhode Island epic told through simple buildings that all speak sweetly about summer life on the Ocean State's shore.

William G. Low house, McKim, Mead & White, Bristol, 1887. Photographs by William G. Low Jr. from the collection of Kathryn and William Low.

The Barnacle, Charles L. Bevins, Jamestown, 1886.

OVERLEAF: Inn Beach, Weekapaug.

VOLUNTOWN
41°35
41°30
41°25
41°20
STONINGTON
WASHINGTON
HOPKINTON
RICHMOND
CHARLESTOWN
WESTERLY
MISQUAMICUT
SHUNNOCK
EXETER
KING
PETTA
Hopkinton City
Nawgoog Pond
Long Pond
Wordens Pond
Passquissett Pond
Cockampaug Pond
Pawawget Pond
Quonoquontaug Pond
Ninigrit Indians Lands
Pawcatuck Bridge
Watch Hill Light Revolving in 1½ minutes
Route of the Steam Packets from New York to Newport and Providence, Daily. Passage 14 to 16 hours.
E½ N. 20 miles from Watch Hill Light to Point Judith Light

BAYRIDGE
MUSCOVY RIDGE

Watch Hill

Two short English words, Watch Hill, succinctly describe this town. The name dates to the seventeenth century, when its hills were strategic lookouts for Native American tribes and European settlers to observe approaching ships and potential threats. It's that same corrugated topography and watery edge of harbor, cove, and beach that make this picturesque town a perennial draw.

Set on the westernmost prong of the state, between ocean and the scoop of Little Narragansett Bay, Watch Hill has long exemplified New England elegance. Like Avondale, Misquamicut, and Weekapaug, it is a borough of the anchor town, three-hundred-year-old Westerly. The land between these hamlets is largely undeveloped, despite nearly two hundred years of growth spurred in 1837 by the opening of the New York, Providence & Boston Railroad. Boat-borne visitors continued to visit, but the daily arrival of crowded trains brought many more people to Watch Hill. Wood-stoked locomotives chugged into the modest Westerly depot where horse-drawn buggies waited to take passengers for a bumpy two-hour dusty or mud-spattered ride to the growing resort town of Watch Hill.

At first a scattering of grand hotels emerged on the open hillsides. Characterized by high mansard roofs, dormers, and spindly verandas, they dominated the town, as recorded in grainy photographs. Bearing no-nonsense names, the first was Watch Hill House followed by Atlantic House, Plimpton House, Columbia House, Narragansett House, and the grandest, The Larkin House. Rare were more evocative names like the Mastuxet Lodge. The 1868 Ocean House, reborn in 2010, captures their elegance with wide verandas, croquet court, and dining rooms—a glimpse of Victorian hotel life.

At the turn of the twentieth century, the town tore down a row of fishing shacks and shanties that clogged the harbor's edge, opening the view to the curved waterfront. Large summer houses appeared among the hotels as the well-to-do took advantage of the hills that offered water views and cooling breezes. Houses ranged from boxy cottages to elaborate shingle style residences. Although the shingle style is most prevalent, sprinkled into the mix are half-timbered buildings, including the diminutive town library as well as some Mediterranean villas sporting red tile roofs. Until recently, down a driveway off Ocean View Highway sat a Pepto-Bismol pink Bermuda cottage. I always slowed down to peer at it, amazed that such a house existed in the New England landscape.

Many houses were designed by architects whose names are now lost, but fashionable architects also contributed their talent. In 1899 Boston-based shingle style maverick William Ralph Emerson built the symmetrical Pinecroft, which shares its front yard with a massive glacial boulder. New Yorker Grosvenor Atterbury concocted the 1913 masonry Sunset Hill high above town overlooking the Rhode Island shore, the Connecticut shore, and New York's Montauk Light. And gleaming with pride of place, Holiday House, designed in 1930, reigns over 700 feet of rocky waterfront with unobstructed ocean views.

America's oldest carousel, The Flying Horse, still turns. The Watch Hill Yacht Club sits atop piles in the harbor in its third shingled guise since I first went there for summer dances in the 1960s. The Watch Hill Chapel faces Ocean House. Originally a finial-capped confection, in 1928 it was reborn in a white colonial revival clapboard cloak. But inside it is still all carpenter Gothic—smooth timber studs and rafters embellished with octofoils, brackets, and ceiling rondelles. The altar and organ have been recently restored in a livery of cobalt-blue paint. "The Church is Many as the Waves, but One as the Sea" is emblazoned in gold leaf among other mottoes and decorative motifs. Along Bay Street, shops open onto covered sidewalks shading diners spilling out of the Olympia Tea Room and St. Claire's Annex.

The allure of Watch Hill has brought the famous to this seaside village. Benjamin Franklin fished off the nearby beaches while setting up Rhode Island's first post office. Other political families, then and now, quietly make the area their summer address. In the 1960s, composer, socialite, and philanthropist Rebekah Harkness ran a noisy dance studio out of Holiday House, now home to singer Taylor Swift.

Watch Hill trails off into Napatree, a mile-long ridge of dune and sandy beach that forms the southern edge of the harbor. Within memory of some longtime residents, it was dotted with shingle style cottages that were torn away by the Great Hurricane of 1938. Now a public beach and peaceful wildlife refuge, it reaches out like an arm hugging Watch Hill to the sea.

A Topographical Map of the State of Rhode Island and Providence Plantations,
James Stevens, 1831. Detail of Westerly, with Watch Hill at the far left.

BAYRIDGE

For years, I have ridden my bicycle past this house, which sits on a corner wedged into a slope in Watch Hill. Shading the house from the morning sun is a two-hundred-year-old gnarled silver maple as gray as the weathered cedar shingles that wrap this gambrel-roofed cottage. The maple was one of five that lined the road in front of the house. Two were brought down by the Great Hurricane of 1938. Hurricane Bob tore another out in 1991, and the fourth simply laid down during a storm beside the typical Watch Hill cobblestone wall. The property is just under two acres and runs down the hill to a dock that gives on to Foster Cove.

When the house was built in 1900, it was half its current size, with porches that wrapped the north, east, and west sides. A wealthy New Haven banker nearly doubled its size by enclosing a number of them, creating a veritable lexicon of outdoor spaces—screened, glazed, or simply covered. In one case, he created a grander dining room that expands onto the front porch, adding walnut paneling and finely detailed wood beams.

Three generations have lived in this house, a family with an appreciation for great design and an array of residences in other beautiful places: Bar Harbor, Palm Beach, and, on Philadelphia's Main Line, one designed by architect Horace Trumbauer. The current owner's mother bought the house in 1945 without consulting her husband. It was for sale for the grand sum of $10,000, but the realtor suggested that an offer of $8,400 would carry the day. Since her husband was serving in Hawaii at the end of the World War II, her father purchased the property. She set about modernizing the house, notably by refinishing the dark-green walls of the living room with a wash of white and apple green. The liming still graces the room today, although slightly faded to a blue-gray.

The formality of the first floor is tempered by low ceilings and simple, unvarnished woodwork. Vestiges of the past are still alive, offering a glimpse into a privileged life of years ago, one of housemen, maids, and housekeepers. The butler's pantry is a long, narrow corridor, lined with glass-fronted cabinets filled with dishes and glassware befitting a house of this scale. The kitchen has been lightly modernized and opens to a drying porch and the stairs leading down to the backyard and dock beyond.

The house is constantly being cared for. In the 1950s, a massive kerosene-fired furnace was installed beneath the entrance hall. There is still talk of looking down through an iron grate to the flames below. The aging furnace was held together with metal tubing and wires until it was finally removed in 1970. Pulling up a corner of the area rug reveals a plywood patch that replaced the grate. The care and feeding of this house continue today. The owner's son, an architect, has carefully measured and drawn the house, which was helpful in updating the aging electrical work. During renovation work, a zinc-lined tank was discovered in the attic. Water collected there provides ample pressure for the fixtures below.

What I love about this house is that it so closely reflects the personality of its owners. There is wonderful exuberance in the selection of wallpapers throughout the house. The bedrooms are appropriately papered in florals, floor to ceiling. One bathroom has a jazzy travel poster paper, popping in yellows and blues. But my favorite is the wallpaper of pimento stuffed olives that dance behind the bar, a space tucked under the main stair, frequented by the younger generations summering in town. It's made more festive by a 1960s vintage Pschitt! poster tacked to the door. On it, a smiling young woman holds a bottle of the French soda.

I worry about the future of houses like this, and I am relieved that this one is so loved. It is still a summer house with no insulation, single glazed windows, and the occasional squeak in the floor. Like so many from the past, this house combines cool dark interiors with life lived outdoors on breezy or sun-dappled porches. These idiosyncrasies lend warmth and character—a personality that is difficult to capture in a new, well-insulated, airtight building. It connects to the soul of Watch Hill and a simpler time. The details and imperfections remind you that someone pieced the house together by hand, board by board, nail by nail. Here's to old buildings and the history they keep.

Some of summer's best moments are spent on the porch. Multiple options—glazed, covered, and screened, something for every activity—wrap this house.

L'Orchestre – Puzzle 500
PICTURE PUZZLE

The barnlike profile of the gambrel roof is a classic architectural form defining many summer cottages along the New England shore.

OVERLEAF: Homespun character: white furniture and house trim painted with the same brush.

Time and ocean air have softened the dining room's unfinished wood walls and ceiling, a warm wooden embrace for candle-lit dinners.

The wash of white and apple green over dark blue brings a driftwood character to the living room paneling.

A Campari-red console, surrounded by dancing olives, is the house bar. Colored kitchen chairs speak to the owner's whimsical take on what had been a formal, staffed kitchen.

The greens of summer pervade the house: wallpaper, bedspread, paint, and flowers.

OVERLEAF: Evening comes to the rocky edge of Block Island Sound and the silhouette of the Watch Hill Light.

MUSCOVY RIDGE

There is magic in discovery—finding a corner restaurant tucked away in a familiar part of town or coming across an overlooked row of charming houses on a road you thought you knew. I felt a frisson of mystery approaching this shingled cottage for the first time, off two roads I regularly travel, and in sight of a house I recently designed. How had I missed it? Though near the main road leading into Watch Hill, it is emotionally worlds away, buffered by copses of trees and reedy wetlands. A private world.

The road bears the name of the farming family who built the house roughly 125 years ago. Approached from the road on a curved double-track driveway through a thicket, the house is sited on a bump of land above six acres of woodlands and salt marsh. A simple wood bridge connects to a forested island. There are telltale signs of a ferry landing along the waterfront—a stone retaining wall that might have formed a pier, remnants of a waterborne connection to Pawcatuck, Connecticut, across the bay.

Little of the house has changed; its silhouette remains almost as it always has been. A persimmon door, tucked into the face of the building under a deep overhang, welcomes guests. Across the threshold is a cozy cottage world. The renovation by architect Nate McBride, a classmate of mine from architecture school, was done with an appropriately light hand, creating an environment that eloquently speaks to the owners' desire for a home resonant of Rhode Island summers. His wife, interior designer Kari McCabe, revived the core of the house to its original, tobacco-brown wood, all centered on a brick hearth. It's easy to imagine sinking into a deep chair by a crackling fire. Dashes of color, comfortable furniture, and a carefully edited selection of rugs update the snug atmosphere.

The warm heart of wood rooms is wrapped in a collar of white painted spaces. On the water side is the lawn porch, where, in addition to small ensembles of furniture, McCabe reinvigorated the space with white painted walls and pale-gray painted floors. She introduced built-in benches at each end to accommodate dining or groupings of chairs and tables for sunset cocktails. The white room reflects light into the core of dark wood rooms behind. Formerly an open porch, it is now glazed in with windows on three sides, a summer room with views of woodlands and the Pawcatuck River estuary.

As in so many houses built at this time, the kitchen was designed to be used by domestic staff, a warren of unusable spaces including a dark butler's pantry blocking views of the water. These rooms were opened to one another, creating an eat-in kitchen with a large breakfast table under a bank of windows. A small porch for drying linens and staff use was turned into a mudroom located off the corner of the building, painted white like the lawn porch.

Rarely seen in new houses is exposed wood framing, the character-laden skeleton of a summer cottage. Here, post and beam, planks, and exposed ceiling joists add an old-fashioned character just this side of rustic. Adding to other quirky moments is a fold-down shutter, hooked to the ceiling, that separates bar and living room. And a sly winding stair, also shrouded in timber, winds up to the second floor and a kinked hallway meandering to the bedrooms.

McBride expanded the second floor by enclosing a sleeping porch, a feature that has all but disappeared. In the days before air conditioning, these porches, usually on the second floor with at least two exposures, offered the hope of snagging a bit of air movement on hot summer nights. This one has become a second-floor office for the owners. The bathrooms maintain their original porcelain fixtures, white painted boards, and vintage character.

Outside is a new south-facing bluestone terrace, which takes advantage of three exposures—east toward the front lawn, south into scrubby woodlands and the island, and west across the marsh to Little Narragansett Bay. A stand of limbed up tupelos, squiggled by wind, filters the view toward Connecticut.

The house has benefited from the recent addition of heating and cooling, enabling the owners to extend the summer. They now open the house earlier in the spring and linger longer into autumn and Thanksgiving. Longer shore life is a not-so-secret wish of every summer resident.

A persimmon door, green window sash, and white trim on the red cedar shingle wall that tucks into the front of the cottage.

OVERLEAF: Above the front lawn amid shrubs and flowers, the house rides a wave of glacier-formed knoll.

A once-open porch has evolved into a family gathering space, all white and replete with chairs and furniture of many vintages.

The rounded river rock on the chimney is typical of garden walls and foundations in and around Watch Hill.

Deep exposed joists cap the kitchen.

Dinner al fresco—life on the screened porch.

Nook or cranny? A twin bed tucks neatly into a second-floor dormer.

A schooner model moored on the stair landing. Some of the best parts of these cottages are hidden, tucked behind walls.

A flip-up mirrored panel pins to the ceiling, opening the bar to the living room.

In the tobacco-brown dining room, Windsor chairs surround the dining table beneath a hovering paper light.

OVERLEAF: Tupelos, shaped by coastal winds, frame the view of Little Narragansett Bay and a house I designed a decade ago.

NUSHKA HOO

Weekapaug

If you hop on a bicycle in Watch Hill and head east, in about six miles you hit Weekapaug. You can ride along Atlantic Avenue, a straightaway that passes the state beach and hotel-studded Misquamicut. A more leisurely rolling ride runs through the woods along Scenic Route 1A, passing the grand Second Empire house at Langworthy Farm that marks the turn to town. Long ago, the Langworthys would open a gate, but now you follow Winnapaug Inlet arriving in the town whose total commercial district comprises a summer sandwich shop and town hall, known here as the Fire District Office.

"At the End of the Pond" is the translation of the Narragansett word Weekapaug. But which pond? The small town of summer and a few full-time residents is squeezed between two: Quonochontaug and Winnapaug. These ponds are fed by inlets formed by stone jetties that jab into the Atlantic and bookend the village. One is near the sandwich shop. The other separates town from neighboring Quonochontaug at the far end of a stretch of barrier beach and nature preserve.

Shortly after the Civil War, the town began to shift from farm to summer colony. Old photographs capture a few farmhouses set among modest board-and-batten cottages and large shingle style buildings. Large or small, the houses are wood inside and out and carry the scent of cedar and the slap and clatter of screen door and wooden steps. Smaller cottages dot the Fen, a former grazing pasture, now a swampy home to turtles and redwing blackbirds. A parade of larger residences—the Gray Ladies—along Wawaloam Avenue commands ocean views over sloped lawns. A German spy is rumored to have hidden in the attic of one of the largest during World War II. Grander houses perch on Weekapaug Point and above massive Gull Rock. More recent designs, some modern, tuck into the woods farther inland. Weekapaug has avoided the spotlight of neighboring Watch Hill and remains a quiet, low-key community.

There's a sense that the past is near, a feeling borne out in old property deeds. Some prohibit hog farming, tanneries, rendering, beer saloons, the storing of gunpowder or coal, and other signs of a bygone time. No forge furnaces or anything to do with the production of iron, perhaps due to Thomas Edison's short-lived attempt to magnetically extract iron from the sand on Quonochontaug's barrier beach. Several properties still maintain the right to harvest seaweed.

In the early 1960s, Weekapaug's last boardinghouse, the Rockhaven, came down, leaving the grand Weekapaug Inn as the only hotel in town. Founded in 1899, it stood on the beach that still bears its name, Inn Beach. At first it was a modest shingled guesthouse with thirty rooms, but it grew three times in size, becoming a more complicated collection of sheds, boathouses, and a dormitory topped by a giant wood water tower. The 1938 hurricane wiped it away along with a dozen or so cottages. In June 1939 the new Inn opened a quarter mile back from the sea. It stands today, a grand shingle style building with colonial touches, porte cochere, and oxblood shutters.

In 2010 the Inn was reborn as the epitome of beachside luxury, updating what was a charming anachronism. Previously, rooms were cooled by opening a window and closing a louvered door to the hallway, encouraging cross ventilation. There were no televisions; a single lobby phone booth served guests. Coat and tie were required at dinner. The Inn did not serve alcohol, but guests could store their own in open cubbies—mixers were supplied for evening cocktails. It was a glimpse of privileged shore life in the 1930s.

The Weekapaug of my youth was similar—no air conditioning, the rare television. Though the yacht club was slightly more than a wooden shack on stilts, there were dressy evening dances. We learned to sail in beamy Beetle Cats, America's oldest wooden one-design sailing class. A man driving a truck, scale swinging off the back, delivered produce. In the morning, neighbors gathered to pick up their mail at Lamb's General Store.

This is where I learned that buildings are layered with history, memories, and texture; that shingle style cottages were best with expansive porches and, Cape Cod style or modern, all should blend harmoniously into and capture nature. They are never just structures.

Weekapaug, in the center of this map, pokes out into the Atlantic, pinched between two saltwater ponds and their barrier beaches.

NUSHKA HOO

When my wife, also an architect, and I discovered a piece of land atop Weekapaug's highest ridge—an impenetrable scrub of brambles and invasive vines filled with rabbits, turkeys, and roving coyotes—we knew we had found the perfect spot for the house we wanted to build for our family.

The land had been sliced off the original Chapman farm, a once-sprawling, nearly treeless expanse crisscrossed with stone walls leading down to the Atlantic and Quonochontaug Pond. In clear sight was the blue horizon, Watch Hill, New Shoreham on Block Island, and the tip of Long Island. It was a strategic vantage point. In the late 1930s, the U. S. Army built two tall fire towers. I always thought they were to watch for forest fires, but it turns out they were there so that soldiers could direct fire from local gun emplacements to enemy ships and submarines trying to slip into Long Island Sound. That explains why our neighbor's house is called The Barracks—it housed soldiers manning the lookouts. Friends of mine remember the towers. They were torn down when an adventurous boy fell from one and broke his arm. But the concrete foundations were still there when we cleared the land, along with hundreds of boulders, some the size of pickup trucks.

I never wanted to design my own home. It seemed like a busman's holiday, and I could barely imagine becoming my own client. I spend my days designing for wonderful clients from as near as a block away to as far as Bangkok, fulfilling my creative spirit. In the end, just as with any house design, I took it one step at a time, looking at the history of great Rhode Island houses. Two came to mind. One, renowned—the William G. Low house that sat above the water in Bristol, designed by McKim, Mead & White. For those who study the shingle style, almost no house is as famous. The second house was an unknown bungalow, Periscope, in the neighboring hamlet of Haversham. Somewhere in the blend of these two buildings was our house.

We sited the house perpendicular to the road to catch more sun and built a suite of rooms in a separate building—guest room, garage, watercolor studio—defining the western edge of a green front court. I borrowed the Low house's elongated gable silhouette. The Haversham bungalow inspired the hipped porch that spans the full eighty feet of the south facade. In lieu of traditional columns, six broad slices of shingled wall support the porch roof, each nipped off at angles radiating from the center window. Twelve feet wide, the porch shades and adds living space to the first floor. Bay windows tuck under the overhangs at each end of the house, admitting light into the kitchen and first-floor bedroom suite. Flat-roof dormers and a prow-like balcony add space to the second floor. Replacing the Low house's spindly brick chimneys, one large, center stack pins the house down.

A sheath of western red cedar shingles and nearly black Seal Harbor green trim lets the house fade into a revived native woodland and meadow. The property welcomes back wildlife that scattered during construction. For those considering native plantings, it works. The property teems with beautiful birds from goldfinches to a great horned owl and animals like squirrels, foxes, and a silent, nocturnal bobcat.

To capture an older cottage vibe, we chose an interior of wood—dark and cool during the day, glowing caramel at night. We all but banished plaster board. Kitchen, bathrooms, and the solar, a medieval term for a second-floor living space, are paneled in planks painted seafoam green or the warm white of a traditional sailboat. The hall, a name used by early shingle style architects, is our main living and dining space. Five woods grace the room: mahogany paneling below a frieze of diamond-cut yellow cedar shingles, quarter-sawn white oak floor, and pine windows all below a limed poplar ceiling. A scant coat of finish oil lets the wood breathe; no thick varnish separates your touch from the wood. Bedrooms sport different species, giving each a distinct character: white oak, red cedar, or vertical grain fir. The staircase is lined—walls, ceiling, and railing—in planks of pine. The exposed wood gives the house a distinct aroma, as though the carpenters walked out the day before.

And there are other architectural references. An exposed steel beam in the living space honors Stanford White's steel-beam-supported ceiling at his own residence, Box Hill in St. James, New York. The glass-and-mahogany screens that create the inglenook around the fireplace are borrowed from the Isaac Bell house in Newport. Like that house, double-hung windows come right down to the floor, an idea also taken up by A. Hayes Town, a Louisiana architect whose work I admire for its vernacular simplicity.

The furniture has been cobbled together from estate sales in Weekapaug and grand Newport houses. Twelve arts and crafts dining chairs were rescued shortly before the demolition of a neighbor's 1885 cottage. Wicker furniture abounds, and a ship's clock from a Newport sale chimes every thirty minutes. There's meaning in every selection. This house has deep South County roots, over sixty years of memory brought to life in physical form.

A Dutch door and windows between the screened porch and the kitchen allow for conversation between the rooms.

OVERLEAF: The broad sweep of Low house is the inspiration for the south elevation. Angled shingled piers continue the cloak of cedar down to a seating knee wall.

A view down the eighty-foot-long front porch with exposed rafters supporting the roof. A curtain wall of double-hung windows brings light and views into the living room, also known as the hall.

The screened porch is painted the same Seal Harbor green as the window trim. As a delicate synapse between indoors and outdoors, this porch is the most popular room in the house, spanning from early spring through Thanksgiving.

Five different wood species make up the interior surfaces of the hall. The plate rail with its cedar shingles above pays homage to houses of the 1880s while the wicker furniture brings summer into the house. Oriental carpets and Victorian tables also speak to that era.

OVERLEAF: Cork floors and a pale institutional green remind me of kitchens from the 1930s to the mid-century.

WEST

JOHN SINGER SARGENT
RATCLIFF

Eclectic objects: A diorama of arrowheads hangs above a chest from a house built in 1876 less than a mile away; the lamp came from travels in Italy thirty years ago. In the dining room Stickley style chairs, a Moroccan rug, and a plate from a Napoleonic volume of Egyptian architecture complement each other.

Next to the powder room sink, a 1930s tourist map shows the roadways and airplanes of an earlier time.

Each guest bedroom is lined in a different wood—here, Douglas fir under a limed wood ceiling. The rug is from a recent trip to Rajasthan.

A trio of overscaled double-hung windows brings a golden glow into the hall.

Strips of vertical-grain western red cedar wrap another guestroom. The ceilings are set at an early New England height—a cozy seven feet above the floor.

Mahogany screens, fabricated on site, enclose the fireplace snug. The 1830s glass comes from a recently demolished house in Mystic, Connecticut.

The tile above the fireplace was influenced by the turquoise-blue Tiffany glass fireplace surround in the Veterans Room at the Park Avenue Armory in New York.

OVERLEAF: A dock on stout piles leads to a float in water just deep enough to clear a motorboat propeller or sailboat's centerboard.

NORTH

FOSTER
SCITUATE
JOHNSTON
PROVIDENCE
CRANSTON
Pawtuxet
Pawtuxet River
Hope Furnace
COVENTRY
WARWICK
Warwick
WEST-GREENWICH
EAST-GREENWICH
Topham Hill
EXETER
NORTH-KINGSTOWN
Wickford
North Ferry
RICHMOND
SOUTH-KINGSTOWN
Little Rest
South Ferry
Tower Hill
Charles River
CHARLESTOWN
HOPKINTOWN
Pt. Judith
Beaver tail
Light House
CONNANICUT I.
PRUDENCE ISLAND
RHODE-ISLAND
Portsmouth
Middle Town
NEW PORT
BARRINGTON
WARREN
BRISTOL
Mt. Hope
Mt. HOPE BAY
Bristol Ferry
Howland Ferry
MASSACHUSET
KENT COUNTY
KINGSTON COUNTY
ATLANTIC OCEAN

PERISCOPE
NINIGRET FARM
EASTCOTE

Haversham

At the age of nine sailing aboard a tidy, thirty-two-foot sloop approaching Mattapoisett, Massachusetts, I learned that nothing is better than arriving by sea. At speeds slow enough for a minimal wake and to make safe landing, the shore approaches gently across the reflective surface, quietly sliding by, rotating as the dock nears. Before that trip, on the Cunard liner *Queen Elizabeth*, I felt the same magic cruising into Southampton, England, after a five-day Atlantic crossing. Knowing the land from the sea gives you a perspective you always attach to a place, however long you know it.

That's how I feel about Haversham. Knocking about on Quonochontaug Pond or racing to the finish line in a fleet of sailboats, it was a mysterious forested bank. Along the cove, a ring of barnacle-covered rocks protruding from the water made getting near tricky. More ominously, submerged boulders, seaweed gently pulsing with the currents, were an additional hazard that made me think twice about approaching. I had friends who lived in Haversham and neighboring Shelter Harbor. They would appear at the yacht club in Weekapaug in their Beetles or arrive by Boston Whaler. But I never saw their houses, adding a mystery that wasn't unlocked until I visited friends there many years later.

My perception was right. It is mostly woods and forest. Hundreds of acres of it, some gently sloped, some choppy hills, have been designated as wildlife and nature preserves. The faded asphalt roads are bumpy and buck along with the topography, becoming sandy lanes and driveways near the pond. The specks in aerial photos are houses, and they vary greatly—farmhouses and asymmetrical shingle style cottages with covered porches. There is at least one arts and crafts residence and in between are new houses, designed to sympathetically join their neighbors. The large properties assure everyone's privacy. It is a quiet hamlet that brings together the best of country life and connection to the saltwater coast. Walking the leaf-strewn paths, it feels as if the Narragansetts are nigh. Indeed, signs of their time here, arrowheads and pottery shards, are occasionally unearthed, and in one area still stands a ring of stones. Whether it is was a ceremonial location or a primitive paddock is largely a matter of conjecture.

The woods are filled with erratics—boulders left in the woods by the ice sheets. It explains the rocks out in the water—glaciers weren't picky about where they went or what they left behind. The shore is rocky, but the view across the pond features the sandy bar, green with beach grass and Scotch pines, that is the inland side of the barrier island. The Atlantic sparkles beyond. In between pass scores of small craft—friends out for a morning sail, powerboats towing water skiers, and anchored skiffs out for an afternoon of fishing. And sometimes, in the heat of a race, sailboats beating to windward, their skippers too busy to look across at the shady shore.

The State of Rhode Island compiled from the Surveys and Observations of Caleb Harris, Harding Harris, c. 1814. Haversham is in the center of the north shore of Quonochontaug Pond.

PERISCOPE

The bungalow. The very name conjures a modest home, its deep porch under a fold of sheltering roof. India birthed the bungalow in the nineteenth century, a few decades before this simple house type landed on our shores. Bungalows in the United States take on more guises than any other house form I know. In the early twentieth century, California architects Greene and Greene created quintessential arts and crafts examples in the Pasadena hills. Albuquerque and other New Mexico towns are dotted with adobe bungalows, from territorial to pueblo style. In Florida, a stick style island type abounds, with board-and-batten walls and exposed rafter tails. Rhode Island's version puts on a shingle cloak with all its associated charm. A favorite of mine is the house called Periscope, its name a play on the owner's surname, Perry, and its perch, rising up in a meadow with views to Block Island and, as the owner claims, Suriname on South America's north coast.

The Perry name and Rhode Island history have been intertwined since 1644 when Edward Perry moved his family here from Sandwich, Massachusetts. Perhaps the best-known ancestor was Admiral Matthew Calbraith Perry, who served in the Pacific and led the expedition that opened up trade with Japan in 1854. Later, another family member, Charles Perry, invited Frederick Douglass to stay at his house in Westerly several times while Douglass was traveling up and down the Boston Post Road championing the abolition of slavery.

In 1917 the owner's grandfather and a few of his friends and neighbors built the house called Periscope. I envision lean men in plaid shirts and dungarees sitting on stacks of lumber in the open field. Their bungalow defines a summer cottage, an inventive cacophony of studs, planks, beams, doors, and windows of every sort—old school, cobbled together from found wood and reclaimed objects. Their homespun solutions can be seen at every turn. Old wooden lobster buoys crisscrossed with rope become a second-floor railing. A jerry-rigged pulley system opens and closes a high demilune fanlight. Awning windows on the first floor, hinged at the top, open up to the ceiling. It's a two-person job: one person stands on a chair holding the window while another fastens it to a long dangling hook.

Yet this is no flimsy structure. It is anchored to the site atop a massive boulder that pokes through the floor forming the living room's eight-foot-wide hearth and supporting a wall of random coarsely cut ashlar stone. Opposite, a continuous window seat wraps the space like a wooden belt under picture windows that look out across the deep porch. Sturdy timber beams span the room.

This house defines togetherness. In a way, there's no place to hide, but there are corners to cozy up with a book, play board games, and huddle over jigsaw puzzles. It's not a place to keep secrets. Bedrooms in the loft are separated one from the next by an eight-foot-high wood screen wall, all open to the umbrella-like roof. And the house is filled with bits and pieces of life at the shore. A line of horseshoe crabs, a gallery of painted wood boat transoms, belaying pins from the whaling ship *Wanderer* and another in iron from the *Granville R. Bacon.*

The wraparound porch with its overhanging eaves and parapet railing is a cool shady space. Two shingled rooms adjoin it, internal extensions of the outdoor area. One is a bedroom and the other the dining room. A slight step down from the living room indicates that these two rooms were once screened porches. I have enjoyed dinners, and many a cocktail, on the porch, and it was a major influence on my own house. Just as the porch extends living space into the landscape, a spindly widow's walk extends it into the sky.

The meadow in front of the house is alive with native Indian grass, little bluestem, black-eyed Susan, Joe Pye weed and wild indigo. A rusty anchor and hundreds of feet of chain border a path centered on a stand of pines and cedars at the water's edge. Sometimes I think they block the view and other times I think they are the view, particularly when the golden light of an August sunset ends another beautiful day.

A 1970s thermometer, rack of hats, pine cones, butterfly net, and antique scale in the passageway to the kitchen.

OVERLEAF: Three ways to see the view: from the cottage's massive, covered porch, or from a shed dormer above the beds, or from the widow's walk straddling the hipped roof.

0 20 40 60
-20 80
-40 100
-60 120
°F
TAYLOR

A weathervane angel, hovering above the boathouse, trumpets the morning sun.

One wall of the covered porch has become a gallery of boat transoms. *Cricket* came from the stern of a Barnegat Bay Sneakbox, one of a1920s fleet of boats on Quonochontaug Pond, all of which sported insect names.

A chorus line of horseshoe crabs dances along one of two major beams that span the living room. It's a cool, shady space of wood on wood on wood.

The hearth is the heart of the home. A random granite ashlar fireplace sits atop an existing granite boulder and below an unfinished wood ceiling.

Dining in an enclosed portion of the covered porch, a step away from the kitchen.

Flip-up bedroom windows and screen panels—technology from a pre-air-conditioning world.

The loft space is a laboratory of home-spun solutions—pulley systems to open windows, a lobster-buoy handrail, and a trap door to the living room below.

Never waste a corner.

Vertical pine-board partitions separate sleeping areas on the upper level.
The open walls encourage ventilation on warm summer nights.

OVERLEAF: An anchor is attached to chains that border the grass path down to the pond.
The native meadow attracts wildlife from butterflies to birds, ground squirrels to foxes.

NINIGRET FARM

The most interesting stories are complex and layered, like a Dickens novel; plot lines intertwine, characters disappear and reappear in delightfully unexpected ways. Like an episodic novel, this house and woodland site artfully layer family history, gardens, and charming interiors.

Colonial farmers, the Gavitts, acquired the land in 1731 from Sachem Charles Ninigret, the grandson of the Pequot chief who had helped Roger Williams establish Rhode Island Colony. Hanging in the foyer is a framed facsimile of the illustrated deed that formalized the purchase. The vestiges of the property's farming past form a meandering tartan of forest, meadow, and lawn. So too do remnants of the Pequots. In a dappled meadow stands a tumble-down ring of rounded boulders, a tribal gathering place. The function of this mini-Stonehenge remains elusive, but one can almost hear ancient ceremonies and celebrations, a mysterious presence hundreds of years on.

In 1995 the current owner, a retired interior designer, bought the eighty-three-acre parcel from Gavitt descendants, bringing along her own four-generation Rhode Island history. The owner spends her winters in Florida, having put her Providence-based interiors practice into her daughter's hands. The property was called Ocean View when she purchased it, a reminder that its farmland once opened to Quonochontaug Pond and Block Island Sound.

Cobblestone piers mark the start of the two-track driveway, which gently descends into the woodland, the destination hidden in the trees ahead. The sandy drive leads past a pond, surrounded by blue irises and lily pads afloat on the mirrored surface. A neat, shingled barn with sliding green doors nudges you toward the cottage nestled in the sloped clearing.

White oaks, sugar maples, thickets of sassafras and viburnum encircle the meadow that the house commands. A stone wall defines a neatly mowed lawn close around the building. The owner spends her spring—and summer and autumn—working this border into dynamic green displays from broad-leaved Japanese butterbur to spears of *Epimedium*. Colorful flowers are an added flourish, the seasoning, not the meal, and a curated selection of species ensures interest from early spring until deep into autumn. Tucked behind the house is an orderly cutting garden protected from rabbits and deer by a woven wire and lodgepole fence. Flowers from colorful daisies to dahlias find their way into overflowing buckets left without fanfare on the neighbors' porches.

The house, like the land, abounds in history. Construction was wrapped up in 1776 by women while the men kin were off fighting the British. At least six additions have been made over two hundred years. It is a farmhouse through and through, with green doors, shutters, and trim picked out against white clapboard. Constellations of white climbing clematis billow under the windows, and a cloak of azaleas and rhododendrons frames the front porch.

The simple exterior belies the range of rooms, one cozier and more delightful than the last. Throughout, beautiful surfaces—wallpaper, barn board, plaster, painted wood—give each a distinct character, congregating into a world of comfort and country elegance. When the house was purchased, the interior was all lath and plaster. Chipping a small hole in the ceiling revealed a hand-hewn timber structure. Portions of the house were sagging and not on stable foundations, so the timbers were numbered, dismantled, stored in the barn to be reassembled as the house was put back together. The tobacco-colored beams and columns provide continuity and, along with wide-plank floors, unify the intimate rooms.

Two large rooms are exceptions. One is the new double-height kitchen that replaced a bedroom suite, and the other is a sunroom created by enclosing an open porch. The owner enlarged the dining room, which now seats the entire family. Everything possible was reused: doors and fireplaces, plumbing fixtures, and nearly all the windows. A corner cupboard displays a collection of delicate pink lusterware. Neat patterns of seashells grace tabletops throughout.

This cottage is delightful for summer on the porch or autumn around crackling fires. It is a nine-month house, closed only in the coldest seasons, although I did spend a cozy day there one icy February. And the house will remain secluded. Generously, the property has been put into a trust that protects it from disturbance or development. Added to nearby protected woodlands with their bobcats, foxes, squirrels, and turkeys, this slice of Rhode Island, from the old Boston Post Road to the water, enchants all.

Oak-leaf hydrangea billows out over a retaining wall next to the potting shed. A marble fragment from a Rhode Island department store is set in a world of rubble stone, dry-laid granite, and old concrete foundation. The weathered shingles heap texture on this country vignette.

The potting shed in its world of green.

The front door is tucked under a porch that is lined with a carpenter Gothic fringe. The owner's keen eye for texture and color can be seen in the plantings around the entrance—a sensibility that carries to the interiors of the house. The school bell announces arrivals when she is gardening.

This house has just the right balance of painted walls, old floors, wood furniture, and timber work.

There is no such thing as a short conversation on a porch like this. A short visit to say hello can slide into an hours-long afternoon stay.

OVERLEAF: A rush rug, wicker furniture, and plants inhabit this former porch, now enclosed and double its original nine-foot width. Originally, it was a line of rocking chairs "from the days before anyone served hors d'oeuvres," as the owner likes to say.

The pale pink ceiling and the pressed hobnail-glass vase on the table pick up on the pink lusterware arrayed in the corner cabinet.

The timber ceiling and wide plank wood floors are part of the original house. On a plate rail facing the green front door is a copy of the 1731 deed to the property.

Barn boards, left natural on the second floor and painted on the first, were the original interior finish of the house, making their way up the staircase to the bedroom hall.

Turkey feathers gathered on the property explode from a tôle cone. A hint of white paint on an old door suggests the layering of time in this house.

English wallpaper befitting a nineteenth-century farmhouse. Simple iron latches and hinges are found on all of the doors.

Pink pectin shells from Captiva, Florida, fan out on a trefoil table.
They represent twenty-five years of collecting.

The posts of a mahogany Empire-style bed reach the spring point of the lustrous wood ceiling.
This bedroom was added by Admiral Herbert Omar Dunn, an ancestor of the previous owner.
The room has four exposures, reminiscent of views from the bridge of a ship.

OVERLEAF: The sun sets over the dunes along Fenway Beach in Weekapaug. Granite boulder jetties poke out into the Atlantic at the entrance to Winnapaug Pond's breachway.

FOOD JOURNEYS of a LIFETIME
NEAR & FAR
INTERIORS I LOVE
VIRGINIA WOOLF • GILLIAN GILL
Of Green Leaf, Bird, and Flower
Georgia O'Keeffe Art and Letters
JOHN SINGER SARGENT
RATCLIFF

EASTCOTE

From the cockpit of my sailboat during a Sunday series race, my eye was drawn to a broad white oak. It was trembling, not from the breeze, but from a flock of great blue herons, perhaps twenty, roosting in its branches. They were flapping their wings, I think communicating with one another. Behind the tree, across a field sat a house so beautifully nestled into the landscape that it looked as though it had been there for a century. Despite decades of sailing here, I had never noticed it.

Was it new? Beyond its gray cedar wrapper, it had all the makings of an 1880s shingle style cottage, a rhythm of dormers across its sheltering roof, red brick chimney, shady porch. Most striking was a round, three-story tower on its east side. The building's modest scale was a rare sight in the world of large residences springing up along the eastern seaboard. The pale verdigris trim matched the lichen-covered boulders, giving it a soft, lightly bleached quality.

Taken with it, the next day, I approached by land on my bike, getting the barest glimpse down a long driveway. In the small community of the coast, it took only a few questions to find out the story. I was delighted to discover it, like Muscovy Ridge in Watch Hill, was designed by my architecture school classmate Nate McBride.

In some ways, the house is a dream. The husband, a native Rhode Islander, had spent summers by the water and wanted a cottage that brought back happy memories. And the wife wanted a house imbued with memory, where the very structure had soaked up the energy of past owners and their guests. The starting point was to keep the old house itself. After all, it had survived the 1938 hurricane, so it wouldn't be right to tear it down now. Of the architects interviewed, McBride was the only one who wanted to keep the old, uninsulated building. The goal was to capture the setting and give the sense that perhaps an architect had only made some minor touch-ups. So I was half-right, the house was both new and old. Its success lies in its deft connection to site and history.

The original cottage contained a small kitchen with no view of the water. It was blocked by a maid's room, vestige of an era when even modest houses were staffed. Jammed against a staircase, the fireplace was something to look at rather than enjoy. A suite of modest bedrooms comprised the second floor; above it, an unfinished attic, and no tower.

Removing the maid's room doubled the size of the kitchen, giving it south light and water views. The expansion is seamless, a juxtaposition of mellow wood framing and interior designer Kari McCabe's palette of butter yellow cabinets and orange countertops plays beautifully against the cooler green of the exterior trim. Open shelves are stocked with glasses and coffee cups; spices and utensils are tucked into the wood framing. The old wood floors have been artfully patched, creating a space that feels as though it has grown over generations. The expanded dining room now adjoins the kitchen. A large bay window brings south light across the covered porch, while opposite, through a pair of pocketing doors, daylight cascades down a new staircase. Balancing the wood kitchen at the other end of the house, the living room is lined—walls and ceiling—in varnished wood. This room has a slight Victorian quality, as opposed to the raw framing of the kitchen. All first-floor rooms open onto the original wide porch, which now terminates in a round screened enclosure at the base of the tower.

Light spills from bedrooms into the narrow internal corridor on the second floor. The furnishings and pictures on the walls emote summer life. The stair continues up to the old attic, now a wood-lined bunk room and hang-out space. On the back of the house is a new bedroom that feels like an old enclosed sleeping porch, and nearby, the husband's office opens to the belvedere at the top of the tower. A radiating fan of rafters under the conical roof with painted columns gives this area an unpretentious nineteenth-century character.

Life aboard a boat could be the inspiration for this deep window seat set beneath the arc of an eyebrow dormer window.

OVERLEAF: The south side of the house is all roof—a sheltering architectural gesture that says home. It lands on delicate pale green columns to shade the veranda and terminates in the three-story tower.

Weathered wood and green paint—an exercise in restraint and a peaceful backdrop for the family and their guests to gather.

Exposed radiating rafters on the tower roof suggest the ribs of an umbrella, providing both shade from sun and shelter from rain.

A patchwork of paint and boards suggests nautical signal flags. Their imperfection reflects the casual nature of cottages along Rhode Island's coast.

The living room opens through French doors to the screened porch.
Paneling and details around the fireplace recall houses built in an earlier era.

In the kitchen, painted surfaces—sea green windows, butter yellow cabinets, and gray floor—play off the wood structure of the oldest part of the house.

Simple solutions and old-fashioned technology are still used in this cottage, like the roller shades in the windows above the kitchen sinks and the rope door handle on a cupboard door.

The New VEGETARIAN COOKING for Everyone
cook + book

Mown paths make their way through the dense meadow. Quonochontaug Pond, barrier island, and the Atlantic lie beyond the greenery littered with large lichen-covered boulders.

OVERLEAF: July's evening sunlight sparks boats, houses, and flowers alike.

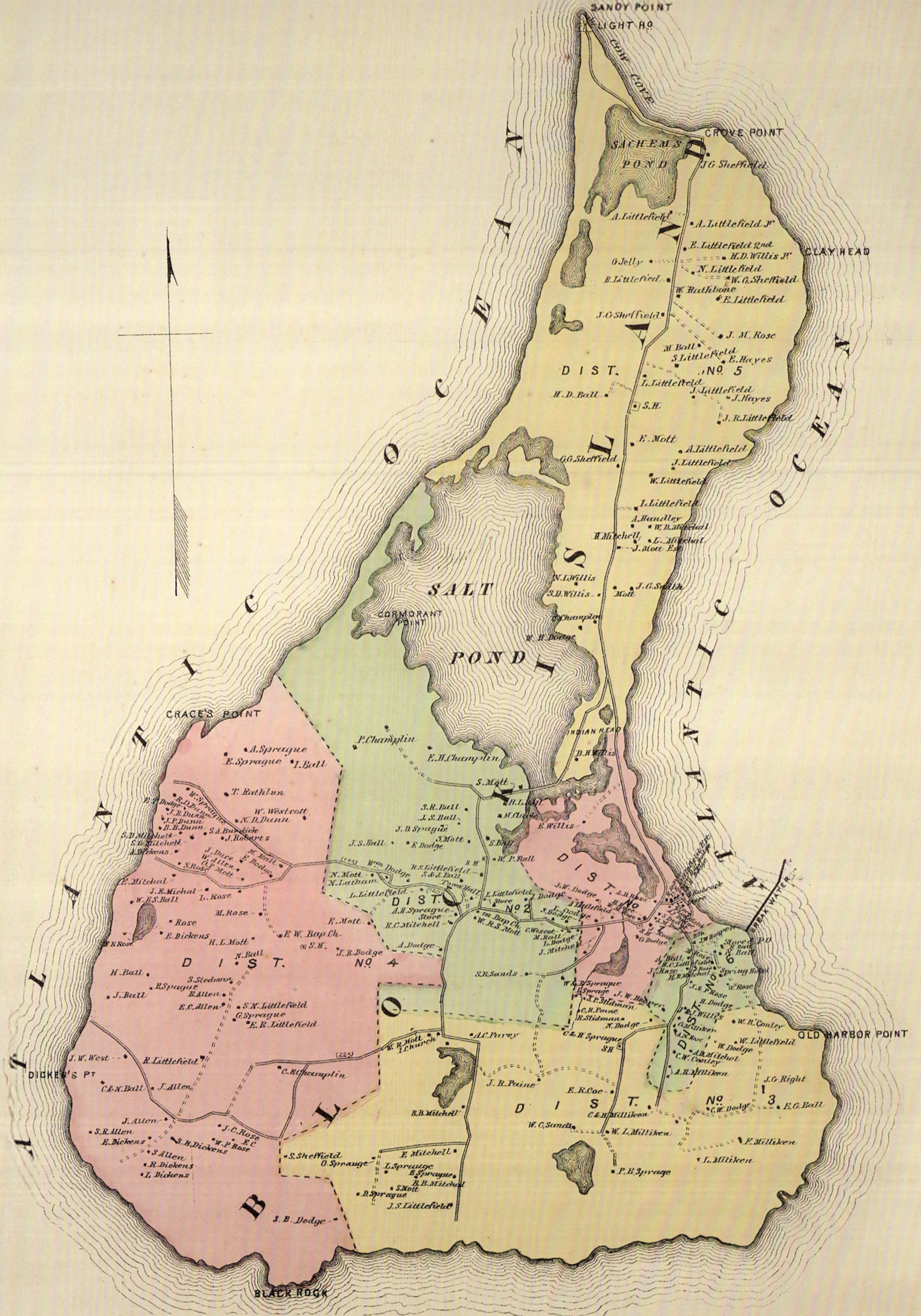

SANDY POINT
LIGHT HO.
CROVE POINT
SACHEMS POND
CLAY HEAD
DIST. No 5
SALT POND
CORMORANT POINT
INDIAN HEAD
CRACE'S POINT
DIST. No 4
DIST. No 2
DIST. No 3
OLD HARBOR POINT
DICKE'S PT
BLACK ROCK
ATLANTIC OCEAN
ATLANTIC OCEAN
BLOCK ISLAND

FIDDLER'S GREEN
CHAMPLIN FARM
RISOM HOUSE

Block Island

In the wake of Henry Hudson's discovery of Manhattan and the Hudson River, fellow Dutch privateer Adriaen Block explored New England's southern shore. Sailing in 1614 aboard *Onrust*, a ship built with the help of the Lenape tribe, Block cruised the coast and discovered that Long Island and Manhattan were islands. He might have been the first European to see the Outer Lands of Montauk, Nantucket, and Martha's Vineyard. Along with his namesake Block Island, it's possible that he also named Rhode Island, calling it Roode Eylandt, Dutch for red soil. In any case, he maintained a lively trade with the local Manissean tribe under an exclusive three-year license from the Netherlands. In 1661 an adventurous group of twelve families purchased the island from the Massachusetts Bay Colony and settled there as farmers and fishermen.

Seen from the mainland across Block Island Sound, the island is ever present, like the moon in the night sky. And, as the moon shifts from crescent to circle, from every mainland vantage point, the island changes shape and appearance. From Watch Hill and Weekapaug it could be mistaken for two separate islands, low gray masses on the horizon. Travel along the coast and the forms draw close until, around Matunuck, the island appears as a single, gentle rise. The weather on Block Island is quintessentially coastal: mild, breezy summers and chilly winters tempered by the surrounding Atlantic. Fog can quickly engulf the island, as I experienced years ago when, walking along a sandy spit, I became disoriented by a sudden summer whiteout.

The Mohegan Bluffs dominate the southern edge, but much of the island is sandy and lies low to the surf. The Great Salt Pond nearly cuts the landmass in two and creates the double-rise look from the mainland. The topography is gently undulating and open, reminiscent of the landscape at Little Compton; about half is protected by nature trusts, including the Block Island Wildlife National Refuge. Common blue violets, white baneberry, and yarrow grow in the sandy soil along the edge of the sunbaked roads. These bumpy lanes make for wonderful walks, or better yet, bicycle rides, hilly enough to get your pulse up, but not so challenging that you can't circle the island on a morning ride.

A half-day sail, an hour-long ferry ride from Point Judith, or twenty minutes by air brings you to the town of New Shoreham. Just as the vegetation and landforms on the island hark back to another time in Rhode Island's history, the main town of New Shoreham seems fixed around the turn of the last century. When one imagines nineteenth-century Watch Hill or Narragansett, I think it must have looked like today's New Shoreham: simple wood buildings, carpenter Gothic details, wooden covered porches. Victorian mansard-roofed hotels, photographed in black and white, could pass for a vintage image of life before the automobile. The first hotel, Spring House, rose in 1854. It's still in business. President Ulysses S. Grant stayed at another, the Oceanview Hotel, during a special session of the Supreme Court. The heritage of these buildings and the guidelines for new construction are as carefully managed as the island's landscape.

Lighthouses punctuate the north and south ends of the island. The blocky North Light, clad in rusticated granite, stands guard over the waters stretching to Narragansett. High on the Mohegan Bluffs, foghorn blaring out to the Atlantic, stands the octagonal Southeast Light. At night its green light flashes every five seconds. It is a muscular brick structure with thick canted walls that brace against the ocean winds. Below it, as though torn from the salt water, lie jagged cliffs and the stone-strewn beach.

Atlas of the State of Rhode Island and Providence Plantations, D. G. Beers & Co., 1870, plate 97.

FIDDLER'S GREEN

A clean take on traditional forms, modern details, and a simple palette make this house an interpretation of the older cottages along the coast. Several requests to consider the project and an invitation to walk the property ultimately convinced Peter Bohlin of Bohlin Cywinski Jackson to take on the design. He delivered a modern Block Island house, one that brings him annually to visit with the owner.

The design reminds me of a clutch of New England houses huddled in the landscape, or maybe a herd of white bison or Conestoga wagons circled on a hilltop. The house is broken into several discrete volumes, masking its true size. The gabled pavilions reduce its scale and create an interplay of inside and out, a green and gray checkerboard of architecture and courtyard. Flat-roofed passageways link the farmhouse-like blocks sheathed in weathered shingles. All skew slightly to the views, relaxing the spaces between, lending the house a subtle organic quality, a fresh interpretation of the quirkiness of many older buildings.

Daylight reinforces the notion that this is a building made up of smaller parts, as though the pavilions were once separated but are now connected by enclosed walkways to create a single residence. Clerestory windows introduce bountiful daylight, dramatically shooting periodic streaks of sunlight as though across a sundial. Slots of space, columns centered in rooms, juxtaposed low and high ceilings—the interior spaces are casual and open. The owner, a graduate of Rhode Island School of Design, selected the light interior palette. The limited range of color values, stained shingles, and trim allows focus on the spaces and shapes within the structure.

Older houses express their structure in boards and timber of Douglas fir, pine, and cypress. Here, in a stark honesty of construction, are exposed gusset plates, rivets, flying beams, rafter tails, and mesh railings. The skeleton of the house reaches out beyond the shingled skin. Where older house structures support the exterior sheathing, here timber beams and columns extend through the wall, forming pergolas and sunscreens.

Steel tie rods span the living room's cathedral ceiling, keeping the roof from doing a split. Stacked, center stage, is a varnished Jenga-like tower of fireplace and a pair of shafts that push through the roof, emerging as dueling stone chimneys. Every room has at least two exposures. Where the second floors of older houses are open to the rafters, giving no privacy between bedrooms, here a diaphragm of glass and wood reaches to the ridge, separating the spaces.

A sense that this house grew over time, pieces added one to the next, makes a relaxed yet organized composition. In fact, the design evolved even during construction. A new ceiling/floor was inserted in the original double-height kitchen, providing space for the primary bedroom suite above. A separate pavilion houses two guest suites.

Paths of crisp bluestone pavers weave through the burnished wooden floors connecting the buildings, linking them to the stone terraces outside. These ribbons of stone add textural complexity and stand up to sandy foot traffic. The stone veneer on the chimneys and foundation walls is squared off and planar but visually related to the rounded rubble-stone walls, remnants of the original farm.

The property abounds in native greenery. A world of *Rudbeckia hirta*, *Echinacea purpurea*, *Baptisia tinctoria*, and the tongue-twisting *Schizachyrium scoparium* surrounds the buildings and extends across the hilltop as a pollinator garden. The house enjoys high views atop Block Island's open fields and bluffs. Paths meander through a patchwork of meadow and brambly thickets of shrubs; remnant stone walls are armatures of past farm life. Views to the boulder-strewn water well below the site tease you onward through green swales and rocky steps down to the beach. The sound of the crashing ocean and briny breeze off the water fill out a picture of life on this fragment of Rhode Island adrift in the Atlantic.

A pair of large granite shards frames the passage through a blocky stone wall into the rolling hills of the island.

The porch tucked into a shallow roof connects the living room block to the rest of the house.

Exposed floor joists, beams, and columns reveal the structural systems of this house in a modern way. Large expenses of glass, floor to ceiling, are divided by muntins to give the windows a traditional sense of scale. Seaside mementos are displayed on a built-in shelf.

Judiciously placed skylights ensure copious daylight throughout the house.

The wood fireplace structure contrasts with the painted surfaces surrounding it. A clerestory window peeks through the opening above.

The clean lines of the kitchen: unadorned ceiling and simple, well-proportioned cabinetry.

The living room is a cathedral to life at the edge of the Atlantic. Its vertical proportions give the space an uplifting scale; the tall windows bring the lawn, water, and sky inside.

ST. BARTHS

View from on high: a bedroom balcony overlooks the island.

Cut bluestone meets a wall of tumbled stone with tailored lawn on one side and a profusion of wildflowers on the other.

OVERLEAF: Block Island's windswept landscape and the Atlantic's rocky shore.

CHAMPLIN FARM

Families discover Block Island for a host of reasons: a friend's invitation, a business trip, or a short holiday stay. A desire for change brought this family to the island. After years of rentals on Long Island's eastern tip, they decided to look farther afield for something quieter. Poring over the *New York Times* classifieds, their eight-year-old daughter spotted a modest Block Island farmhouse for rent. At only eight hundred square feet, the diminutive building was dubbed "The Dollhouse." It was one of a number of buildings on the landlord's property. The daughter grew up spending summers there, eventually marrying and sharing the island with her own family.

When a sixteen-acre farm in rolling hills overlooking the Atlantic went on the market, the owners grabbed it. Not sure of next steps, they mulled over ideas for several years. Eventually they hired a trio of prominent designers: architect Gil Schafer, interior decorator Miles Redd, and landscape designer Deborah Nevins. The brief was simple: a five-bedroom house that was elegant, understated, and everything Rhode Island.

The history of the island is rooted in farms like this one, owned by the Champlin family, who pastured livestock and grew crops like corn and alfalfa. Schafer, relying on the wisdom of the farmers, recommended putting the new structures—main house, guesthouse, and barn—on the existing building footprints. After all, the farmers had worked the land since 1780, and they had generational knowledge of the wind, sun angles, and views to boat traffic. Working within these parameters would also help the new designs conform to the island's size restrictions. The result is a grouping of appropriately scaled buildings that evoke the island's architectural past and agricultural roots.

The main house massing is that of a farmhouse that has been elevated with classical detailing and motifs that hit all the right notes: pedimented entrance porch on attenuated columns, detailed rake moldings, crisp window trim, and colonnaded porches. Cottage-style six-over-nine double-hung windows flank the front door. Shingle style elements abound; shingle patterns— straight, wavy, fish scale—and walls that curve into a second-floor balcony. An eyebrow dormer and at least three other dormer types enliven the roof. Rather than bright white trim, a soft, off-white paint tones down the contrast with the gray cedar siding.

Redd has decorated several houses for the owners. Here, they wanted a sophisticated interpretation of a summer home. The interiors come together in a soft palette, ranging from creams to the palest of pink and light blue. The entrance hall floor is weathered wood, with textured walls of overpainted grasscloth. The newness of the ground-up construction with its crisply detailed millwork and cabinetry is softened by the patina of antique furniture. Flat weave rugs anchor the rooms. The bar is paneled in reclaimed white oak, and its gently faded appearance looks as if there is no applied finish at all. The stair hall and passageways are lined in the kind of painted boards found in older houses, but here they have been set into a lightly classicized architectural framework. The roofscape is evident in the second-floor bedrooms where the sloped ceilings come down low, recalling older Rhode Island cottages.

The landscape retains the history of the site, holding on to the old farm feeling. Native grasses and tall sedges are woven into a pattern of paths and stone walls above a view of the ocean. The renovated barn is part of a stone-walled pool enclosure, the structure now serving as pool house. Stone steps set into the grass descend the hillside toward a pond on the property. A verdant amphitheater made up of stone seats and native grasses introduces a subtle geometric structure where the hardscape and plantings meet. Nevins carefully anchors the house to the land, creating a feeling that the building had always been there. During construction, care was taken to protect a giant elm that stands near the main house, a sentinel from generations ago. More delicately, climbing roses scale trellises attached to the shingled walls. These intersections of plants, terraces, stone walls, steps, and house are reminders that the landscape can be the defining aspect of any home.

A shed extension nuzzles into a bank of hydrangeas. Climbing roses thread through the weathered trellis, a charming motif found in cottages throughout the islands off the New England coast.

The main house and guesthouse overlook pond and ocean. The landscape moves from tailored to wild: a stone wall at the house, stone steps set into the lawn, and native grasses leading to the water.

Tapered spindles support a winding mahogany handrail as it descends, coming to rest on a turned newel.

Light reflects softly off beautifully painted woodwork. The screen door rails and stiles echo the panel layout on the front door.

Open shelves stocked with white and blue dishes, baskets, and vases line the walls of the white-on-white kitchen. The conical brass pendant light centers the room.

The bar is lined with character-grade wood, knots and varied grain patterns that give the room a relaxed quality.

Soft colors, a shore-inspired palette, tie the house to its island environment.

A painted white tester bed slips cozily under the sloped ceiling.

A white-columned porch wraps the house. An array of shingle patterns adorns the walls of this island retreat.

RISOM HOUSE

This house sits on its open wood deck as a midcentury wooden chair might sit on a patio overlooking the ocean. And for good reason: famed Danish furniture designer and Knoll Furniture co-founder Jens Risom built this house in 1967. A native of Copenhagen, Risom made New England his home in 1939, choosing to live among like-minded designers and their modern houses in New Canaan, Connecticut. Perhaps his earlier life on the Baltic drew him to Block Island, thousands of miles across the Atlantic. The grassy site and salt air might have reminded Risom of the Jutland Peninsula's horizontal landscape.

The house bridges traditional shingled cabins of yore and postwar flat-roof and plate-glass houses, the clean, uncluttered open plan yielding a beach house of modern efficiency. The prefab house, components fabricated in Massachusetts, was built for less than $25,000. Barges ferried panels, windows, and other pieces from Point Judith to New Shoreham. From the pier, trucks rumbled across the landscape to a waiting foundation. Construction on the island and its logistical complications slowed the schedule from an anticipated two months to a still-speedy four.

Not an A-frame, but close to it, a clean, folded shingle roof shelters a double-height room with loft above. Missing are the typical details and flourishes of a classic shingle style or Victorian cottage. Besides a small kitchen and living area, two bedrooms and a bathroom occupy the first floor. They are on the closed, inland side under what was originally an open loft lit by a lone skylight and large triangular window. Risom divided the loft to incorporate two bedrooms as his sons grew, turning the cottage into a four-bedroom house. Opposite is the main event: the twenty-foot-tall wood and glass curtain wall that captures the sea and sky. In the double-height space is a box of black steel placed against a fireproof metal shield, a Scandinavian take on the American Franklin stove. It connects to a lone red brick chimney that rises through the space, piercing the roof.

Risom moved beyond an austere machine for living, marrying the warm wood interiors with shingle style roots. Taking cues from Danish design, bold colors and simple wood-laminate cabinetry set in a Mondrian-like composition fill the great room. But rather than the primary colors of Mondrian, maize, turquoise, and vermilion punctuate the wood interior. The floor of this room slides out under the glass wall to the deck through the diaphragm of glass. Truly, this house makes good on the adage about form and function.

The family continues to enjoy summers in the compact house, a focal point in the New England landscape. A clean sensibility organizes the whole composition—house, deck, lawn, hedges, view, concentric rings of indoor and expanding outdoor space. This careful arrangement reveals the methodical mind of the designer and his ability to turn that organization into well-considered beauty. A faded yellow "R" hangs on the inland shingle wall. With this initial, like a chop on an Asian print, Risom seems to have signed off on this love letter to family and site.

The cottage and its contents are all of the midcentury era—multigenerational family ownership has kept the house intact.

Glass and more glass. With a twenty-foot-high transparent membrane between inside and out, nothing obscures the view to the ocean.

A bicycle shed mimics the cottage, its yellow door a match to the R on the mother ship. Both express a simple, unadorned symmetry.

R
Risom

The grand space, a room of many functions, is a gallery of midcentury life, the walls a curated clutter of daily life.

The main event, a two-and-one-half-story window wall, is divided into a grid of mullions and muntins, sliced by the sheltering A-frame roof.

Sea-smoothed pebbles from the beach. Nothing in the house feels extraneous, and all has been collected with a keen eye to simple beauty.

THE BIG BOOK OF THINGS TO DO AND MAKE

A skylight over a desk offers a view without a dormer protruding from the cottage's prism-like silhouette.

One of the beds and its Marimekko pillow in the sleeping loft. This small cottage can accommodate a surprising number of overnight guests and family members.

A Risom-designed chair and ottoman in a glassy corner of the main space. Rusted industrial artifacts hang on the wall.

A modest stair climbs to the loft above.

OVERLEAF: The Atlantic from the deck. Periodic trimming keeps the ocean from disappearing behind the greenery at the top of the dune.

SACHEM PON
HAM

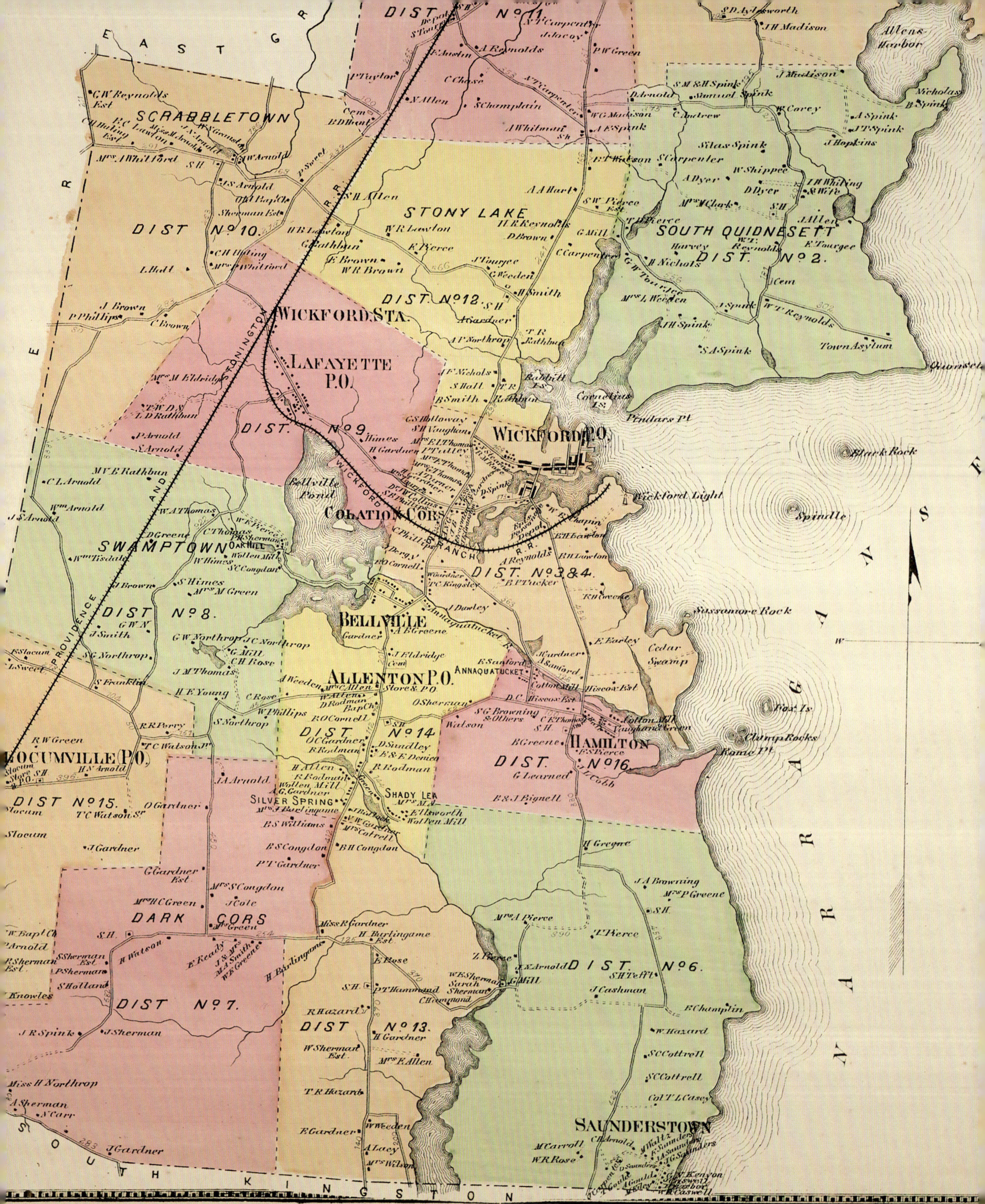

EAST GR
SCRABBLETOWN
DIST Nº 10
DIST Nº 11
STONY LAKE
SOUTH QUIDNESETT
DIST Nº 2
DIST Nº 12
WICKFORD STA.
LAFAYETTE P.O.
DIST Nº 9
WICKFORD P.O.
Allens Harbor
Town Asylum
Rabbit Is.
Pendars Pt
Black Rock
Spindle
Wickford Light
Bellville Pond
COLATION CORS
SWAMPTOWN
OAK HILL
DIST Nº 8
DIST Nº 3 & 4
BELLVILLE
Sassamore Rock
Cedar Swamp
ALLENTON P.O.
ANNAQUATUCKET
HAMILTON
DIST Nº 16
Fox Is.
Clump Rocks
DIST Nº 14
SILVER SPRING
SHADY LEA
DIST Nº 15
DARK CORS
DIST Nº 7
DIST Nº 13
DIST Nº 6
SAUNDERSTOWN
SOUTH KINGSTON
PROVIDENCE AND STONINGTON R.R.
WICKFORD BRANCH R.R.

Saunderstown

I can't tuck a dollar bill into my wallet without thinking of Saunderstown. The first president peers from the bill's oval frame, an engraved copy of painter Gilbert Stuart's famous unfinished portrait of George Washington. Saunderstown was Stuart's boyhood home when he still spelled his name "Stewart" and before he moved to Philadelphia to paint Thomas Jefferson, John Quincy Adams, Dolley and James Madison, and many famous artists and important figures.

The Stewart house is red clapboard, built in 1751. The long gambrel form ends with a wooden undershot waterwheel. Across a rocky waterfall, attached to a barn, is another waterwheel. Both spin stones that ground local tobacco leaves into snuff.

Saunderstown was home to a host of artists, writers, and architects. John La Farge, muralist and stained glass competitor of Louis Comfort Tiffany, was also a resident. His son Christopher Grant La Farge and Philadelphian George Heins formed the architecture firm Heins & La Farge, designers of New York's Cathedral of Saint John the Divine and the first stations of the IRT subway system. Around 1896 La Farge also designed Saunderstown's much smaller Chapel of Saint John the Divine, a shingle style church with a simple roof and steeple topped by a painted belfry. For the sum of $2,200, the chapel was erected, four years after the larger Manhattan cathedral. In 1903 La Farge designed the town's diminutive Willett Free Library. Clearly his success beyond Saunderstown had not diminished his love for this small town.

Other buildings of extraordinary personality graced Saunderstown. Some are long gone, including a small inn called Holiday House Hotel. It was a long extrusion of mansard roof and simple comfort, a syncopation of shed dormers protruding from its steep roof. Tacked on one side, with the simplicity of a week-long amateur construction project, was a screened porch looking out across the scrubby landscape. More substantial was the clapboard Casey Farmhouse. A photograph from 1925 features the house on a gentle rise. A massive brick chimney punches through the pyramidal roof and below it spring four almost comically small dormers, one to a side. A row of Doric columns marches across the front loggia, giving the house a stately demeanor.

The town's 1902 shingle style Baptist Mission church is now the post office. The shingle walls and arched, tripartite openings in the belfry are now hidden under a sheath of white clapboard. A metal finial atop the tower is the only element left of the original church, suggesting an opportunity to restore the building to its shingle style roots.

The town connects to the literary world as well. Edith Wharton frequently visited her cousin Frances Willing Wharton, daughter of writer Benoni Lockwood. Owen Wister, the father of the American western and author of *The Virginian*, lived here. And though not a native, musical composer and playwright George M. Cohan summered in Saunderstown.

Saunderstown is enchanting. The town sits on Narragansett Bay's Western Passage, about a third of the way down Boston Neck, the land spanning south from the Annaquatucket River to Point Judith. Set into a mature woodland, the town hugs the Bay's rocky shore. Towering pines, oaks, and other mature, high-canopy trees protect its inhabitants against the elements. Separating properties are piles of rhododendron, bushy mountain laurels, and massive clethra. The town was purchased from the Narragansett by the Saunders family, early settlers and ship builders. They lent their name to the town, which seems to have barely made it out of the nineteenth century, let alone the twentieth.

Atlas of the State of Rhode Island and Providence Plantations, D. G. Beers & Co., 1870, detail of plate 103.

THE COTTAGE

Across a verge of grass, set in a rubble wall, are two green posts, sharp as pencils. There used to be a gate between them, but it's gone now, and a shaggy wall of rhododendron and bay laurel says what the gate might have, something between "keep out" and "welcome in." Once through the wall, you descend through a curving tunnel of green, branches knit above you, sky barely visible, to emerge through a mass of ferns and clethra. A wooden bridge crosses a mossy cut, stream trickling below. It is an intimate landscape that wraps around you as if you'd hiked the greenery up around your shoulders like a cloak.

In the tight clearing, it's almost hard to tell where woods end and house begins. But, tucked under a block of second floor is the front door, recessed in shadow. The owner thinks this is an awkward entrance, but I think it's charming. Her grandparents designed the cottage and built it with the help of a local builder, creating a house whose coziness echoes the intimate setting. All the first-floor rooms open directly and gracefully to the sloped site. Cleverly, this was made possible by changing levels within the house itself, with steps between rooms to negotiate the changes.

In fact, "Granny" designed the house from the inside out, and she thought it was the ugliest thing she'd ever seen. It is a family cottage overlooking Narragansett Bay across a grass terrace and knee-high retaining wall. Below, tucked into the cliff, is Bathhouse Number 4. The previous three were washed away by hurricanes. Swimming here is off the wood dock; the beach is too rocky and craggy to even allow wading.

Earlier generations anchored boats in the bay, reached by launches tethered to the dock. Though the boats are gone, they live on, painted on green trays hung on the walls inside the house. Sailboats include the grandfather's motor sailor ketch *Green Pastures* and his schooner *Bagheera*, named for the panther of Jungle Book fame. A model of *Bagheera* rides across the living room mantel. Other trays feature her father's sloop *Still Waters*, a yawl called *Sea Fever*, and a gaffe-rigged cutter called *Carillon*. Watercolors of naval scenes link to her father's skippering minesweepers during World War II.

Unfinished mahogany panels the main level. Mellowed to a tobacco brown, the wood is fancier than the caramelized pine that sheaths the second floor. The floors throughout the house are vertical grain fir. A shipwright employed by the builder fashioned the timber ceiling in the living room, but most others are more modest, covered in the least pretentious summer cottage material—painted homasote—basically a thick cardboard. The furniture has been assembled from family houses as they have been sold off, each piece imbued with family lore.

"One of the things I have learned is that it's best when colors don't match," says the owner, perhaps channeling her grandmother's do-it-yourself spirit. And although she claims nothing in the house goes together, with a natural sense of beauty and an eye honed by a career in charge of continuity on movie sets, she has created a home of casual charm. Her handmade backgammon board, simple boxes nailed together by a local carpenter, is lined with cork and embellished with stylized wrens. She was the one who painted the boats on the metal trays. And she brushed two shades of green on the wicker chairs in the sunroom. A flower-filled vase is her grandmother's tennis trophy. The upstairs bathroom, once green with white trim, has flipped to white walls and green trim, its curtains repurposed cotton hand towels.

And I disagree with her grandmother. This is a beautiful cottage. Its massing is well-organized, a hierarchy of big and small forms. She and her builder friend managed to thoughtfully arrange the gabled shapes, starting with a colonial-simple main block; twin dormers and sunroom extension combine in an unpretentious but sophisticated massing; the green trim and white sash bring a light graphic quality to the elevation. Standing on the dock and looking back at this house, I am captivated by its down-home, matter-of-fact charm.

The owner created this backgammon set by painting a simple wooden box put together by a carpenter friend. Wrens keep an eye over the game's progress.

OVERLEAF: The charm of the house comes from its composition of simple repeating forms—porch, gables, and dormers echo one another.

A simple wooden bridge along the path to the front door.

Windows and screen doors in the sunroom provide the barest of separation from the surrounding world of grass, trees, stone wall, and bay.

A board-and-batten bathing pavilion is pushed tight against the retaining walls of the property just above the waters of Narragansett Bay.

Weathered bluestone floor and faded board ceiling. A day bed and its wicker cousins invite conversation and contemplation in this indoor/outdoor room.

JOHN IRVING
A WIDOW FOR ONE YEAR
YANK BROWN FORWARD
STONE
WILLIAM FAULKNER
THE REIVERS
HURRY SUNDOWN
VOLUME ONE
K.B. GILDEN
DOUBLEDAY
HURRY SUNDOWN
VOLUME TWO
K.B. GILDEN
DOUBLEDAY
THOMASINA
PAUL GALLICO
BATTER UP!
QUARTER BACK BATES
SCOTT TUROW
PRESUMED INNOCENT
John Gardner
Leon Uris
Armageddon
DOUBLEDAY
NICHOLAS AND ALEXANDRA
ALL THIS, and HEAVEN TOO
Rachel Field
Speak to the Winds
Ruth Moore
Penny Candy
GONE WITH THE WIND
MITCHELL
MACMILLAN
THE LEOPARD
Pantheon
SWISS FAMILY ROBINSON
WHEN A MAN'S A MAN
WRIGHT
THE ROOM WHERE IT HAPPENED
JOHN BOLTON
The Miracle of DUNKIRK
Walter Lord
Viking
THURBER
Rumer Godden
THE GREENGAGE SUMMER
FOSTERS RUSSIAN BANK
UNCLE TOM'S CABIN
Two Years Before The Mast
Dana
THE FORSYTE SAGA
GALSWORTHY
SCRIBNERS
KEEP THE CHANGE
THOMAS McGUANE
SKETCHES BY BOZ
BARNABY RUDGE
T.B.PETERSON
HARVARD COLLEGE CLASS OF 1940
25th Anniversary Report
1965
1975
1985
Bush's Brain
WAR AND
JOAN DIDION
THURSTON CLARKE
The American Coast
ALONG THE MAINE COAST
THE WORLD OF FARLEY MOWAT
BECOMING
NEW ENGLAND HARBORS
TREASURY OF AMERICA
JOHN MARIN
COASTAL RHODE ISLAND

Generations of summer reading.

The staircase disappears behind a wall hung with hand-painted tôle trays depicting the original owners' sailboats. French doors can close one space from another.

The wood countertop in the butler's pantry provides a soft surface that reduces the risk of breaking plates and glasses. To the left of the glass door cabinets is a swinging door into the dining room.

The sounds of waves, seagulls, and passing boats can be heard through the dining room's open windows. Nighttime brings twinkles of light from houses across the water.

The leafy green tunnel leading from the front gate introduces a world of native New England plantings.

Steps and stone path to the dock where bathers can dive into the salt water.

OVERLEAF: Fishermen are dwarfed by the boulders lit up as a summer day comes to an end.

Sango Point
the Brothers
White Rocks
Connonicut Point
Updykes Harbour
Pinders Point
Cold Spring Rock
Duck Cove
Plumb beach Pt.
Fox Island
Half-way Rock
Weavers Cove
Cranston's Cove
Gould Island
Coddington's Point
Cove
Connonicut
Island
North Ferry
West Ferry
Bishops Rock
Taylors Point
Coasters Harbour Island
Blue Rock
Dutch Island
Great Creek
West Ferry
East Ferry
Rose Island
Dyers Point
Foxhill Cove
South Ferry
Beaver Head
Foxhill
Goat Island
Fort
Newport
Dumpling Rocks
Brenton's Point
Battery
Rock Ledge
Mackerel Cove
Pond
the Bonnet
Castle Hill
Whale Rock
Light House
Old Newtown Rock
Beaver Tail
Brentons Reef
Brenton's Key
Price's Neck
Gooseberry Island
Seal Rock

THE BOULDERS
THE STUDIO
CLINGSTONE
WAINWRIGHT COTTAGE

Jamestown

Conanicut Island sits squarely in the Western Passage of Narragansett Bay, between the Jamestown Bridge and the Clairborne Pell Bridge to Newport and Aquidneck Island. A rocky edge along the water rings the northern shore of the island with the town of Jamestown on the east facing Newport.

Charles L. Bevins is Jamestown's most famous architect. Born in Manchester, Bevins practiced near Liverpool before moving to Newport. Though Newport was the big social draw, Bevins's clients chose a quieter, more rural life on Conanicut. Bevins rarely held back. His houses are a panoply of architectural elements, bordering on the fanciful, each characterized by a distinctive personality and silhouette. They are an agglomeration of towers, terraces, porches, verandas, eyebrow dormers, cascading staircases, and a lexicon of windows and trim. Bevins's houses still pepper the island's landscape, dotting rocky knolls, sprinkled among trees, or sitting in open fields. They sport names like Horsehead, The Barnacle, Harbor Entrance, and Channel Bells, also known as The Ramparts, imagery as evocative as the designs themselves.

Conanicut divides into two lobes linked by the arc of the Mackerel Cove causeway. South of the cove the road eventually emerges from the woods onto the mowed grass field of Beavertail, the island's southernmost tip. Surrounding the field are giant exposed stone striations, weathered phyllite, and schist. They are bleached at the top, craggy, splintered, and black with seaweed as they slip under the water. Waves swirl and crash up the rocky crevices, washing over the slanted stone. The water is crystal clear—the sloping sandy bottom fades from turquoise to deep ultramarine.

The 1856 Beavertail Lighthouse, a six-story tall granite tower, marks the mouth of the bay. A knot of whitewashed brick lightkeeper's house and outbuildings flank the lighthouse, brought up tight against offshore winds and the occasional rogue breaker. The lighthouse replaces earlier beacons that have stood on the point since 1712, when the wooden Newport Light became the third lighthouse in the British colonies.

Navigation charts indicate a necklace of more than twenty lighthouses ringing Narragansett's rocky edges, estuaries, and islands. Given all the hazards along the jagged coastline, no beacon is far from the next. From Beavertail, one can spot the lighthouses at Castle Hill, Point Judith, and Rose Island. But, to the west, only a pair of lighthouses guide sailors making their way across the waters, a recipe for groundings and wrecks. Old photographs in the Beavertail Lighthouse Museum show vessels of all types and tonnages, beached in the sand or rolling in the surf, often shrouded in soupy fog.

I remember arriving as a ten-year-old on one such morning on Weekapaug's Fenway Beach, surprised by a blue ketch stranded in eighteen inches of water. In 1922 a similar fate befell *Taro*, a luxury steamer rumored to have been owned by architect Stanford White. In the little-known Battle of Point Judith, the U. S. Navy sank a German U-boat after it had torpedoed an American collier. The steamship *Onandaga* dwarfs these vessels. Wrecked in 1918, the 275-foot-long steamship went aground off Watch Hill; drive shafts, boilers, perfume bottles, and motorcycle parts still litter the seabed. The scattered cargo of other wrecks reflected America's history: wooden lath from Maine, crates of salt from Nantucket, barrels of molasses from the Caribbean, bales of cotton from Savannah.

But the great majority of boats safely make their way through these waters. The lighthouses are built in a range of architectural styles, their names evocative of the New England coast. Conanicut, Nayatt, and Poplar Point Lights are clapboard-clad and house-like. Others are lone brick spark plugs surrounded entirely by water—Plum Beach, Hog Island, Sakonnet Point, and Conimicut. Most are painted white, but sometimes a black base introduces a giant graphic presence, a daytime counterpoint to the nighttime flashes of light. And more than keeping mariners safe, these buildings are often homes, adding another layer of Rhode Island's domestic architecture.

A Topographical Chart of the Bay of Narragansett in the Province of New England, Charles Blaskowitz, 1777. Detail of Connonicut Island.

THE BOULDERS

This house rambles. It's a run-on sentence of gables, bay windows, porches, and domed towers—an elegant architectural cacophony. If not for a wrapper of red cedar shingles and flow of lichen green roof, it looks as though the house might shake apart at the seams. But it's unfair to judge what we see today. When completed in 1888, Charles L. Bevins's design included a belt of deep covered porch that cinched the composition together. At some point, to brighten the interior, one of its owners removed the portion shading the entrance facade. Today a pediment over the front door ghosts the original design and does a fine job of announcing the way in.

A successful anonymous bid at an online auction brought The Boulders into the current owner's life. Though the house and property had been cared for, there were opportunities for improvement. He first tackled the overgrown, two-and-a-half-acre site, enlisting a herd of thirty goats. Like the billy goats munching on tin cans in a vintage cartoon, a hungry 170-pound adult will stop at almost nothing, feeding roughly every forty-five minutes. I imagine a carpet of them moving across the property, a roving flesh and blood woodchipper clearing everything in its path. They spared a tall white pine and a few other trees but, in ten days, the site was chewed down and open. The goatherd loaded his woolly accomplices into a reconfigured school bus dubbed the Goat Tote and they were off, mission accomplished.

A call to the Garden Conservancy brought some experience and help in creating a pond in a natural bowl revealed in the newly shorn landscape. Native plants now thrive on the bumpy property. High above, on a boulder-studded rise, sits Bevins's house. Ironically, when it was completed more than 130 years ago, the landscape was as bare as that left behind by the goats. Vintage photographs show the nearly treeless farmland with the arc of Narragansett Bay beyond the hills. Trees have since grown in, but the view remains spectacular.

The exterior of The Boulders is pure American shingle style, an inventive melange of 1880s design moves that cloak a Victorian core. Only the tall, corbelled brick chimneys hint at the stylized interior. The entrance hall energetically expresses the stick style through its cross bracing, refined timber details, and beadboard panels. The newel post with its overscaled ball finial and incised flower detailing anchors the stair and its spindled railing. A bank of original stained glass windows lights the landing above. The intricate millwork of the hall sits on a floor of geometric wood patterns. Father Time, in a swirl of gray beard and stars, peers out of the oculus in the rough-cut stone fireplace. The portrait might be painter William Trost Richards, perhaps by his daughter Anna or by Richards himself.

The living room is picked out in fretwork spanning the octagonal window seat. English arts and crafts tiles accent the fireplace, and a mirror looks back at the stair hall. Through a wide opening is the dining room, anchored by a master stroke of a sideboard—a collage of nineteenth-century millwork. Brackets, stacks of sliver-thin drawers, machined rondels, and beadboard support a row of green and white stained glass windows. In keeping with the style, a heavy dining table is supported on massive turned legs. The second-floor maze of hallways and bedrooms continues the first-floor detailing and the collection of fireplaces. All this finery is rooted in Bevins's love of English Victorian domestic architecture. And no wonder.

In addition to original interiors, for the most part, the house retains Bevins's deep porches. They extend the interior living spaces through French doors onto covered piazzas, the 1880s term for porches. In places they are twenty feet deep. Caught in a clash of these outdoor rooms is a small seating alcove, one of the coziest shingle nooks I know. Loggias like these may be the best feature of a New England summer home. At The Boulders, they meander around the house, hugging the old building in a shaded domestic embrace.

A forged-metal figure searches the coast with a telescope from his perch near the entrance to the house.

THE
BOULDERS
1888

A pale green roof, reminiscent of lichen or weathered copper, unites a landscape of roof shapes.

OVERLEAF: Deep shingled piers lend a solidity often associated with masonry arches but in a softer all-cedar sheathing.

THE
BOULDERS
1888

Victorian brackets and beadboard grace nearly every corner of the main rooms and stair hall.

The mudroom ceiling radiates from a center rondel. The doors in the house feature diagonal patterns in keeping with the stick style interiors.

PETER
NESS
1948

Windows above the dining room sideboard borrow daylight from an adjacent room.

Original stained-glass panels in the stair landing shower multi-colored light into the entrance hall below.

Strips of alternating wood species animate the floor in the entrance hall. An octagonal table shares the late nineteenth-century roots of the house.

Freestanding tub and sink occupy the bathrooms
much as beds and tables do in the surrounding bedrooms.

White walls keep the house light and airy and provide
a bright backdrop for the oak windows, doors, and furniture.

Cast-iron strapwork connects the tall chimneys to a tie rod, bracing them against the coastal storms.

The muntin patterns carry across windows and French doors.

OVERLEAF: The Gray Ladies—shingled sisters gathered along the water on a late, moody June afternoon.

THE STUDIO

At the height of the pandemic lockdown, hunkered in a Watch Hill base, my weekends became hegiras around Rhode Island, ventures down alleyways in Newport or twisting dirt roads and private lanes across the state. In December 2020, one such trip ended in Jamestown with a ride poking around the quiet corners of Conanicut Island. Driving along the water near Fort Wetherill, I stopped to look at the sunlight reflecting off a mirror-like Narragansett Bay. Above the cove, emerging through bare branches on the stony headland known as Bull Point, rose the red windows and pyramidal roof of a building I'd never seen before.

Some internet sleuthing led me to the owner, whose grandfather purchased the property and its fifty-eight-room cottage, Harbor Entrance, at the close of World War II. Charles Bevins's design for the original house dominated the landscape when completed in 1893. The largest of Bevins's houses, the building had seven levels. A domed tower rose above two giant dueling gables, pinning the composition of porches and balconies emerging from nearly every floor. It was solid, an array of massive stone, timber, and shingle with an elaborately appointed interior. In the 1960s, when houses of this size and refinement could not be given away, the family demolished it. The current owner had spent a part of every year of his life on the property and now watched the yearlong demolition from his roost in a neighboring one-bedroom cottage. Harbor Entrance "was filled with a serenity that fell victim to a more callous age," as he puts it. Trucks trundled off with mahogany paneling, framing, windows, and doors, leaving behind 750,000 pounds of rubble, brick, stone, and a chunk of the old foundation. In 1968 the land was divided among family members leaving the owner of The Studio with the foundation, a well, and the cottage. A new building on the property would serve as a studio for his glass fabrication business, housing layout spaces and a workshop.

It took twenty years to obtain the building approvals needed, and construction finally started in 1990. Financial bootstrapping and the slow acquisition of salvaged materials extended construction to a decade-long crawl. Architect William Crane helped in the design of a building fabricated from a litany of salvaged parts: steel casement windows, an industrial stair from a Providence hospital, red pine timber from Fall River mills, glass block, hand-hewn barn beams from Rhode Island, old steel beams, oak doors, and cornices from New York City mansions, Mexican mesquite doors discovered in Santa Fe warehouses, and granite block from the original house.

Despite the plethora of disparate materials, a taut building emerged. The owner's interest in sacred geometries and proportional systems crystallized the house into a building of elegant form. Tall windows with stucco surrounds are pushed deep into the shingled base. Above it, the band of red casement windows I saw from the cove gives the effect of a clerestory under the overhang of the hipped roof, classical despite its modern language. The design owes a debt to French designer Pierre Chareau, Egyptian architect Hassan Fathy, and Charles L. Bevins, as well as a family friend, industrial designer Alexander Girard.

Combining the capture of daylight and seaside sounds, the house channels energy from its site high above the water. In the owner's words, "Light was ever evident through the extraordinary vistas, always varying, emotional, subtle. Sound was another constant, always changing—the wind, sea, bell-buoys, birds, and ocean vessels." The building is a sort of light sieve. Daylight enters at the top through a cupola and the giant red windows. From there, it passes through a glass-block panel in the floor to the main level, whose entire floor is a grid of glass. From there the light travels to the lowest level, the owner's workshop. His work encompassed sandblasting, acid etching, custom lamination and thermal arc metal spraying for glass installations worldwide.

Ten years ago, the glass-fabrication atelier became a house. Decks off the kitchen and upper floor look far out over Conanicut and the surrounding water. The perspective is unlike any other I know of in the state. From The Studio's vantage point, Fort Adams far below, across the Eastern Passage, loses the power of its thick, granite-walled presence. Newport and its church steeples look like a village in a model train set. And the scads of passing boats are miniaturized. The isolated site is about the senses, the house a prism gathering sunlight, wind, scents, and sounds of the shore.

Etched glass in shapes taken from French curves was the owner's first attempt to create glass art as a student. It is set into the floor with other glass block that lets light into the workspace below.

The Studio rises in the saddle of Bull Point, a peninsula that pokes out into Narragansett Bay, giving it views south to the ocean and north up the Eastern Passage.

The bay is alive with sailing craft like this sloop passing in front of Hammersmith Farm in Newport.

Cedar shingles connect this modern house with the deeply rooted shingle style of nineteenth-century Rhode Island.

Reclaimed doors off a landing on the way to the outdoor stair leading to the bedroom above.

The covered porch on the second floor offers views of the rocky outcroppings in the waters around the house and the Claiborne Pell Newport Bridge in the distance.

Loft space, often synonymous with urban life, provides an airy, eclectic domesticity. Light pours through the glass block above and the over-scaled windows.

william
david
laurie

Philodendrons and other plants, some more than twenty years old, take over a wall in the main space.

A photograph of the owner's mother as a child along with knickknacks and mementos.

Four-square windows wrap all walls of the voluminous bedroom, itself an apartment within the house. Views include a glimpse of Clingstone.

A sheet of acid-etched, aluminum-suffused glass depicts William Morris's Willow Pattern.

Bunches of dried garlic from annual crops grown on the property.

CLINGSTONE

When is a house a dream? A mirage? This fabled building hovering above Narragansett Bay is probably both. No sailor or casual day tripper can ignore this house clutching the stone island beneath. Its iconic silhouette is all overhang, eave, and bands of porch—a house both balanced and precarious. Anticipation builds in the four-minute ride from the Jamestown pier. Stepping off the launch onto the tossing floating dock, the house looms above, a shingle style lodge rising from one of the granite islets awash in Narragansett Bay, known as The Dumplings. A jumble of stone steps through the grass and shrubs leads to the front door tucked into a deep rubble wall under the mass of house.

Twelve months of construction started in 1904 by Philadelphia financier and president of Harrison Safety Boiler Works Joseph Lovering Wharton. He purchased property on Conanicut and built a ramp and loading dock. From there he ferried materials and laborers to a new stone-and-timber pier planted on a field of submerged rocks, the staging area for the new house. The pier lasted until the 1938 hurricane sheared it from its footings, dumping it into the water. The house, unlike others close to the water, survived the storm. Some say the shingle interior aided in its durability, a house that flexed with the storm's pounding. Concussions of guns fired from nearby Fort Wetherill during World War II cracked the plaster of buildings in the area but again, Clingstone's wood interior suffered no harm. Wharton's wife died in 1944, leaving three sons who bickered over money, finally abandoning the house. The 1954 hurricane was no kinder but not intense enough to do any real damage. In the ensuing years, the house fell victim to campers and random visitors hiding out in the building, vandalizing the structure and stealing the remaining furniture.

In 1961 the current owner's father bought the shell for $3,600 in back taxes. At that time, from on the rocks below the house, the sky was visible four stories up through the decayed roof. Turning it into a home became an obsession. The new owner's future wife refused to marry him unless he promised to carry family photos, not Clingstone, in his wallet. Bringing it back to life was a never-ending project. Family and guests alike pitched in. Work weekends were common and included neighbors and friends who were willing to come up, cut boards, and drive nails. The cost of a visit was spending a few hours reviving the old house.

The design knits the shingle style to the American arts and crafts style prevalent in the first decade of the twentieth century. Its shallow roof slopes, deep gable, and balconies echo those of Greene and Greene's Gamble House, but in eastern seaboard gray rather than Pasadena warm browns and khaki. The soft, weathered patina of gray shingle and unpainted exterior trim carries through to the interior. A climb up a tight stair opens into the triple-height stair hall. It, along with the dining and living rooms, is wrapped in time-softened shingles. A balcony wends its way in and out of view, connecting a random rhythm of bedroom doors. Farther up, a cutout in the ceiling teases with a glimpse of the third floor beyond. This spin of wood and space, Piranesi in cedar and oak, hints at the complexity of the building and invites exploration.

A lion, witch, and wardrobe sense of an old house surprises at every turn, down corridors and up staircases. A ship's ladder on the third floor leads through a glass hatch to the widow's walk, a vertiginous experience heightened by the lack of a railing. A windmill overhead, successor to several blown off the roof, provides backup power to recently installed solar panels.

Eleven bedrooms scattered around the house offer guests panoramas of Newport and Jamestown, boats and bridges. Visiting painters, perhaps including artist William Trost Richards, known for expansive landscape paintings of New England, influenced the installation of unusually large plate-glass windows. Views out of the house have the scale and composition of such paintings, giant ever-changing waterscapes.

Time spent in Clingstone is somewhere between living in a memory and aboard a wooden sailboat. The house vibrates with the patina of time on every surface and at every turn. The massive circular oak table remains at the center of the entrance hall, the one piece of furniture too big for vagrants to carry away. Sprinkled throughout the house are white missile nose-cone forms from a military auction. A few things, like the top of the dining room table, came from the fabric of the house. It was once the hatch that covered a cistern mounted on the third floor collecting and storing rainwater. Much of the furniture was purchased over the decades from local estate and garage sales. The extraordinary collection is gathered from other houses that may or may not still exist along the coast of the Ocean State.

The role of art is played by windows, each one an overscaled landscape like this view of the rocky edge of Bull Point.

OVERLEAF: The distinctive four-story silhouette of Clingstone atop its jagged island. The twelve-meter sloop *Gleam* sails by, keeping its distance from the tricky waters that surround the house.

12
US 11

The main stair spills down from the second floor. Tacked to the shingled wall are panoramic photographs of Newport and the edges of Narragansett Bay.

The balcony wraps the house, passing windows, walls, and shingled columns and allowing an easy circumlocution with views of the Atlantic and the silhouette of The Studio atop Bull Point.

Two forms for manufacturing rocket nose cones flank the entrance hall fireplace, which shares a chimney with the dining room and living room fireplaces.

Wicker, split-rock fireplace, and shingled wall in the living room.

Many summers worth of reading, board games, and jigsaw puzzles fill the bookshelves of a corner sitting room.

THE LORE OF FLIGHT
AIRCRAFT ARMAMENT
TRANSPORTATION
Motor Sports
RICHARD RHODES THE MAKING OF THE ATOMIC BOMB
TANKS AND ARMORED VEHICLES
THE ENCYCLOPEDIA OF INVENTIONS
POWERED VEHICLES
The Complete CARD PLAYER
COMEBACK
THE SEA CHEST
THE GAFF RIG HANDBOOK
TRIPLE DEFIANCE!
Alphabet TRAIN FLOOR PUZZLE
28 Pieces · 10 Feet Long!
IMPROVE YOUR OWN BOAT
WOODEN TEASER GAMES SET OF SEVEN
Trivial Pursuit
THE WORLD'S GREAT RELIGIONS
Ceramics
BIG BEN
50th Anniversary
1000
TELEVISION
USA
THE SEA CHART
PILOTING
THE MARINER'S CATALOG
COMMONWEALTH
OCEANS IN PERIL
1943
MATRIX
JANE SCOTT
PICTIONARY
THE GAME OF QUICK DRAW!
RUMMIKUB
Fish Stix
UPWORDS
THE 3-DIMENSIONAL WORD GAME THAT REALLY STACKS UP!
BREAD COOK BOOK
WITH ALL DUE RESPECT
Rhode Island
HUMAN DESTINY
Mariner's Notebook
Newport Houses
Art Buchwald
I THINK I DON'T REMEMBER
THE THIRD THE ASSURED
NAPOLEON AND UNCLE ELBY
OYSTERS
Crime in America
Ramsey Clark
Social Register 1978

The galley kitchen blends apothecary, butler's pantry, and curio cabinet into a meandering space of great character.

Glasses and teacups for every occasion are stored in this cabinet, which separates the kitchen from the dining room.

The squat Castle Hill Lighthouse cleaves to its rocky home.

WAINWRIGHT COTTAGE

Compact and simple, Wainwright Cottage is low-slung, as unprepossessing as the gravel road that brings you to the front porch. Its location down the slope from the road exaggerates its modest form and scale. The exterior belies the world inside—tall visitors duck or stoop to enter through the painted shingle entrance, but inside it feels as though the building has suddenly grown. The main room runs front to back, from the windows on the inland side through a glazed porch to Narragansett Bay. The spaces in the house, including its five bedrooms, are warm and layered, honey-colored wood from floor to ceiling.

Rear Admiral Richard Wainwright built the cottage around 1915. Wainwright was second in command on the battleship *Maine* when it was blown up in Havana harbor during the Spanish-American War. He retired to Jamestown, selecting this grassy site across the water from the U.S. Naval War College. During the Great Depression, the current owners' great-grandparents bought the cottage from Wainwright's widow. Its location on a sheltered part of the bay allowed them to moor their sailboat and watch the parade of other craft passing by against the backdrop of Aquidneck Island.

Generations, from grandparents to grandchildren, still share the cottage. Its physical layout creates life patterns and traditions. One of them is preparing lunch in the kitchen but enjoying it on the porch served on 1950s-vintage TV tables. The juxtaposition of the painted metal trays and wicker chairs from a hundred years before television sums up the aesthetics of this family. It's not just the objects themselves but their juxtaposition that gives this building its personality.

The living room furniture likely dates from Wainwright's ownership, but other furniture and seaside paraphernalia fill the house in the same way a fisherman's net may catch a variety of unintended prey. In other hands, this might have been clutter, but this is a family with an extraordinary eye for beauty and meaning in every object. Collecting antiques and furniture grew into a business, and items were cherry-picked to display in rooms throughout the house in every nook and cranny. A corner cupboard is filled with majolica, but the everyday china is Vernon Kilns "Homespun" pottery made in California. There is a smattering of additional midcentury objects acquired by the grandparents after World War II. The dining table is Danish modern, the light fixture above it from the early 1960s. The white enameled St. Charles kitchen, though seventy years old, is still called the new kitchen. Conveniently and artistically hung above the stove is a collection of vintage spatulas and utensils, arranged on a painted pegboard panel. By contrast, the owner's bedroom hosts a minuet of cobalt plates, platters, and bottles above a bed covered in a pale blue coverlet and toile pillows.

A painting of a clipper ship hangs above the brick fireplace—the building's sole source of heat. Nautical touches like storage bins with hatches outfitted with flush ring pulls are vestiges of Admiral Wainwright's world. A curved bronze plaque from the *Wildwood*, a ferry that plied the waters between Jamestown and Newport, hangs near a chart of the bay. Over the barn door at the dining room entrance spans a name board with "Wildwood" in capital letters. A vintage running light is now a lamp set behind the sofa. None of this feels cliché—it all feels right.

The cottage is one of a few remaining unwinterized houses on the island, and despite its small size, it has its own, even smaller outbuilding across the road. The one-room cabin is known as the chauffeur's cottage, once sparse quarters for the family's driver. Until recently, his chair, a desk, and single bed were arranged in the modest room. This arrangement is a vestige from a time when families living in houses, no matter how small, still retained staff. It also suggests that a house as good as this one can change with the times and be home to new ways of life.

The glossy white and pink lining of conch shells echoes the colors and sea life in the ceramics tucked into the painted interior of a corner cupboard in the dining room.

Wainwright Cottage is the embodiment of a relaxed life along the Rhode Island coast—the simplest of gabled house forms, its shingle walls sprinkled with double-hung windows and dark-green shutters.

The interior of the screened porch is painted white to reflect light into the house through the large twelve-over-twelve windows. Antique oyster plates dot the walls.

Looking out to the east on a mid-summer morning.

WILDWOO

Burnished wood floors, vertical board walls, and open joist ceilings speak to the carpenters' straightforward handiwork—all enlivened by an exuberance of three generations of collecting.

DONT GIVE UP THE SHIP

Yellows, blues, and greens in the furniture and ceramics are a foil to the warm wood of the dining room walls. The room connects to the screened porch.

A midcentury light hovers over a pitcher-full of white hydrangeas plucked nearby.

Blue cushions and pillows on a window seat. Moments like this are features of so many Rhode Island houses—places to read, enjoy the view, nap, or spend the night.

Ceiling fans and open space above the bedroom partitions allow for nighttime air movement.

OVERLEAF: A Watch Hill evening in golds and blues.

ANSET
BAY
AQUIDNECK
OR
RHODE ISLAND
MIDDLETOWN
VAUCLUSE
GLEN
WEAVERS COVE
CODDINGTON'S COVE
COASTER'S HARBOR ISLAND
SHANTONOMI HILL
FORT GREENE
Light
LIME ROCKS
FORT DENHAM
EASTONS BEACH
SACHUEST BEACH
PURGATORY
HANGING ROCK
SMITH'S BEACH
Fogland Point
Sandy Point
Black Point
Woods Castle
Easton's Point
Sachuest Point
Port Hole
CONRADS CAVE
Ocre Point

Middletown

For a long time, Middletown was a mystery to me. Traveling around Narragansett Bay, I never seemed to stop there. I visited friends in Providence or kicked around the waterfront towns of Newport and Bristol. Those towns center on sailing, a lifelong fascination. In Newport, I was lucky enough to match race in a pair of twelve-meter sloops, one of them the America's Cup winner *Intrepid*. Or I might chill with friends in a much smaller J/22. Sitting on a lawn watching the rhythm of beautiful sailing craft glide around the harbor is one of the few places I can be still.

Bristol is home to America's most famous yacht designer, Nathaniel Herreshoff—Captain Nat. I love the cavernous boat sheds at the Herreshoff Marine Museum where visitors can study half-hull models, examine drawings rolled out on the drafting tables, and stare at walls hung with long, wood French curves. These are evidence of hand drawing and craft in the nineteenth century, my favorite period of American history for many reasons, including the birth of the shingle style, a hint of which is found in Middletown.

A significant contribution to the canon of American architecture lies in a deep-red clapboard house, a large addition to an existing farmhouse built in 1729 by an Irish cleric. George Berkeley, Anglican bishop and philosopher, lived a mere two years in the ironically named Whitehall. The house has a stately symmetrical entrance facade with classically pedimented entrance doors and robustly pronounced window surrounds. In 1874 a young architect named Charles Follen McKim, travelling with colleagues to Massachuetts, New Hampshire, and Rhode Island, visited Whitehall. McKim's photograph of the house is one of twenty-six he exhibited as he sought to document the roots of an emerging American architectural style.

McKim wasn't interested in Whitehall's formal principal facade. Instead he photographed the long sloping roof over the back of the house. This low, gangly fragment of the building with a shed addition and teetering chimney became the inspiration a few years later when he and his partners, William Rutherford Mead and Stanford White, launched their careers building in the picturesque modern colonial style. Starting in Newport just three miles to the south, the new firm initially favored casual compositions for these shingle style houses rather than ones reflecting a Palladian ideal. The link to Whitehall is evident in the elongated roofscape of McKim's 1887 William G. Low house, unconscionably demolished in 1962.

Touring the Bishop Berkeley house was a powerful experience. For me, it anchored Middletown as an important Rhode Island pivot point. The visit to Whitehall opened exploration of the rest of the town that spans Aquidneck Island from the Narragansett's low-lying west shore east to the higher manicured fields and estates on the edge of the Sakonnet River. The story of Middletown, its glacial past, bird habitat, farmland, and winnowing stone walls are typical of other Rhode Island towns.

The town's architecture is a blend of colonial houses and others from the nineteenth and twentieth centuries, many more than I can list here. Boyd's Mill, a shingled eight-vane windmill, was built in nearby Portsmouth in 1810, restored, and moved to town in 1995. The 1856 Hamilton Hoppin house is an exuberant Italianate villa by Richard Upjohn, designer of Manhattan's Trinity Church. Like Whitehall, it looks to Italy for inspiration, but through the lens of nineteenth-century Victorian proportion and detail rather than Palladian classicism. The Lyman C. Josephs house might be my favorite in town. It was built in 1882, during the shingle style's best decade. It is a long structure, as though it has been squeezed from a gambrel roof machine and laid across the landscape. Porch, bay window, rubble stone walls all lie beneath the classically detailed eave. The roof is a backdrop to arched dormers, big and small, all a sweeping hillside gesture.

But when I think about Middletown, what still grabs me is imagining the young Charles McKim, lugging a box camera, most likely in an itchy wool suit. He was doubtless unaware of the future influence he would have in bringing about a new American style. At this stage in his career, a hint of his sophisticated eye can be seen when he recognized the roots of the new style in the tumbledown backside of what was then a moldering 130-year-old house.

Map of Newport County, Rhode Island from Original Surveys by H. F. Walling, 1850 (detail).

BOOTHDEN

Of the houses in this book, Boothden comes closest to the architecture that preceded the shingle style. In 1883 Calvert Vaux, the Victorian architect who worked with Frederick Law Olmsted on New York's Central Park, designed this house for Edwin Booth, who was at the time America's most famous actor. The stylized half timbering, brackets, and X-bracing define this house as a clear example of the stick style.

Months into a search for a summer home along Maine's rocky coast, the owners realized that they wanted a longer summer season, warmer water, and a swimmable sandy beach. Their checklist included a large property for a compound, inviting enough to attract their extended family for holidays and vacations. A *Wall Street Journal* advertisement and a chance meeting with a Newport realtor led them to Boothden. When they arrived, it was a white, paint-sick fixer-upper with a tatty red asphalt roof. The house sits at the upper edge of a six-acre bowl of land that overlooks the Sakonnet, which separates Middletown from Little Compton in the distance.

Debate followed about whether to tear down or renovate the house. Their architect, Providence-based David Andreozzi, understood that the building was too small for the client's vision. However, architect and client felt they owed it to the area's history to keep the cottage. They set about to restore it and upgrade the property without making it so museum-like that it couldn't be enjoyed by large groups of friends and family. The house plays an important role in the town's history and, from time to time, strangers knock to let them know that a relative or friends had once lived there. On learning the house would not be demolished, the previous owner was moved to tears. She gave the owners a sheaf of historic drawings and photographs. Studying them and absorbing the information enabled them to re-create all that might have been lost in a demolition, becoming the seed from which a new, larger building flourished.

Along with Andreozzi, Boston-based landscape architect Keith LeBlanc reimagined the house's relationship to the road, the entrance sequence, and how to open views east across the river. They started by lifting the entire house and turning it twenty degrees counterclockwise. They added low retaining walls to mediate the grade change from the road to the front of the house and removed a crumbling asphalt drive that choked an ancient beech and sliced the front yard in two. A new parking court was moved closer to the road, creating a longer, bluestone walk to the front door, which is on the side of the house. The 100-year-old European beech now sits unencumbered on the lawn, in full view from the entrance and beyond.

On the water side of the house, a half dozen "floating trees" crowded the view. In addition to removing some, Andreozzi bent the house in an open angle that engages a broad sweep of the waterside. The landscape architects carefully echoed the angled house form in a series of terraces and landscape layers dropping down to the river. The few remaining trees are lovingly maintained and bring pools of shade to the gently bowled lawn. One is a giant 150-year-old ginkgo, likely a whip of tree when the house was built. Masses of shrubbery on both the land and water sides become part of the building's composition.

Andreozzi removed poorly designed additions, gutted and restructured the house, adding a third floor and a wing that stretches south. X-bracing details are carried from the old building throughout the new extension. At the front door, flanking "wagon wheel" railings were brought back, a detail gleaned from the old hand-drawn elevations. A new octagonal screened porch anchors the water side of the house.

No record remains of the original color scheme, though historical photographs indicate dark trim and windows. Architect and owners selected a palette of red window sash, gray shingles, and gray-green trim that speaks to a Victorian color sensibility.

The original site felt as much farm as residence. A barn on the road side of the house has been converted to a stained glass studio for the wife. There was a three-bedroom boathouse, blown down in the 1938 hurricane. And perched on the water's edge stood an octagonal, shingled windmill, which survived the hurricane but evaporated in a fire, leaving only its foundations that, for a short time, supported a one-story chicken coop. Today a new eight-sided gazebo speaks across the lawn to the house's octagonal screened porch. It is raised eight feet above the grass and connected by a staircase to views up and down the river, pinning the property to its extraordinary site.

The pyramidal roof with a ball finial and the bracketed columns on the addition to Boothden speak to the stick style character of the original house.

OVERLEAF: The house turns its broad elevation, all windows and porch, to the lawn, capturing morning sun and views of the Sakonnet River and Little Compton.

View across the Sakonnet River to Little Compton.

The entrance on the Calvert Vaux portion of the house has been returned to its original nineteenth-century detail.

OVERLEAF: Doric columns support the roof of the raised gazebo—a departure from the Victorian detailing of the house itself.

Ore Bed
Mashapogue
Pawtuxet
Pawtuxet R
Warwick
Warwick
Aporague
Warwick Neck
Greenwich Bay
East Greenwich
East Greenwich
Potowoom
Hunts R.
Maskechusick Point
Patience I.
Providence
Bay
Bullocks Pt.
Barrington
Palmers R
Miles Bridge
BRISTOL
Warren
Warren R
Papasquash
Bristol
Mt. Hope
Mt. HOPE BAY
Coles R.
Lees R.
Taunton R.
Fall R.
Pocasset
Tiverton
Hog I.
Nahet Pt.
Prudence I.
Part of Portsmouth
Calfpasture Pt
Despair I.
Hope I.
Dyers I.
North Kingstown
Wickford
Black Rock
Fox I.
Conanicut
Jamestown
Gould I.
Coaster Harbour
Rose I.
Goat I.
Newport
Middletown
Portsmouth
Quaker Hill
RHODE ISLAND
EAST PASSAGE
Wantons Pond
Mill
Little Compton
Warrens P.
Seaconet Pt.
Seaconet Rocks
Brentons Reef
Coggeshall Ledge
Seal Rock
White Rock
Beavertail
Light House
Island
Bissels Mills
South Ferry
The Bonnet
Little Rest
Kingston
Tower Hill
NARRAGANSETT

Little Compton

If there is one part of Rhode Island's ocean edge that has maintained a centuries' old character, it is Little Compton. Even in a state as small as Rhode Island, it feels, and is, remote. Getting there requires crossing bridges, wrapping around waterways, and following ever-narrowing roads to the state's green southeast corner. The sky is a dome of blue over open meadows and fields. Roads are lined with wind-frizzled oaks, sycamores, and maples. It's easy to imagine life here 100 years ago. Little Compton's location on the Sakonnet River made it home to sawmills for wooden boats and to salt works necessary to preserve food for the long trade routes to and from Newport.

Modern development has ignored Little Compton. The town reminds me of the Rhode Island of my childhood, when there was a fraction of houses per acre as compared with today. Here, the built world is a sampler of New England building types: churches, saltboxes, granges, and a 1905 water tower border the streets in the center of town. Clad in painted clapboard, shingles, stone, and brick, they are colorful neighbors. And the farms, with their sheds, barns, and outbuildings, all beg to be captured in oil or watercolor.

And they were, by a Little Compton native, artist Sydney Richmond Burleigh, born in 1853. The English arts and crafts traditions boiling away across the ocean dominated Burleigh's artistic life. Embracing the philosophy of the allied arts, he painted, designed furniture, and worked with architects on the design of some of Rhode Island's most interesting buildings. In 1880 he helped found the Providence Arts Club. The clubhouse is an arts and crafts interpretation of an Elizabethan townhouse that would be as much at home in London as it is in Rhode Island's capital. Burleigh's colorful bas-relief plasterwork on the club's street front demonstrates his technical and stylistic range. The influence of William Morris and other contemporary arts and crafts painters can be seen in the willowy figures, crowned with golden halos, overlooking Thomas Street. Floral arabesques, spirals, and bas-relief portraits decorate the panels between the facade's timbers. The clean lines of his elegantly proportioned furniture feature painted and gilded panels in his hand, a nod to furniture designs by Morris and others.

But it is his paintings that so beautifully capture the life, light, and spirit of Little Compton. They romanticize its colonial past. Stylistically, the work ranges from light and airy watercolors to hazy oil paintings. In both media, they reflect their era. The oils nod to French Impressionism. After marrying Sarah Wilkinson, also from Little Compton, Burleigh left to study in Paris. Four years later, the influence of that French style can be seen in his views of the farms and towns. He painted sunny beach scenes, the rocky coast and ocean rollers, town and farm life as well as scenes of people gathered in the countryside. Another subject was the Sakonnet—more bay than river lying off in the distance. His watercolors remind me of paintings by Winslow Homer and William Merritt Chase. The world that poured from his paintbrushes a century and a half ago could be just last year. Or today.

Rhode Island, D. F. Sotzmann, 1797 (detail).

TOWER HOUSE

An 1812 windmill, with its swirling blades and canted walls, was one of a pair that stood near the center of Little Compton. The constant noise of the windmills, grinding grain between granite wheels, wore on the locals until one burned to the ground. The remaining tower was moved, down to the edge of the Sakonnet. In 1886 Judge Thomas Slicer purchased the windmill, by then a wreck housing chickens, for a mere $25, and shuttled it back uphill, plunking it at the edge of a field behind a stone wall along the old main road. He hired the appropriately named Providence architecture firm of Stone, Carpenter & Wilson to incorporate the tower into a new house for him and his wife, Adeline. Slicer, a friend of President Theodore Roosevelt, had been introduced to Little Compton by Sydney Burleigh, and, after renting for a few years, he and Adeline decided to build the cottage.

The compact house wraps around the old, tapered tower like a honey bear hugging a tree, the domed tower just peeking over the ridge of an umbrella-like roof of cedar shingles. The resulting composition could be a turtle lifting its head to survey the farmland and the uninterrupted view to the river, across the fields slashed with gray tree trunks and stone walls. Less noticeable is the "Dinghy," a low Sears, Roebuck and Company mail-order addition that drifts into the landscape behind the house, largely unseen from the road. Although the property is modest in acreage, the unobstructed views give the sense that it is one of Rhode Island's biggest landholdings.

The current owner, one of six sisters, had long shared a different Little Compton house, one purchased by her parents in the 1970s. In recent years, the siblings shared the home on a first-come, first-served basis—first to arrive got her choice of bedroom, the last, the garage. Tired of this stressful arrangement, her husband suggested they look at the Tower House. It had been on the market for two years and was now being auctioned off. They went to see it, and when the door opened, she had an immediate emotional response: "My heart leapt." A last-minute bid netted the house. There were a few white-knuckle months while they anticipated the strain of owning a new house in addition to one in Boston. The other sold just in time to close on the new property.

The building's simple form reflects a straightforward interior and easygoing floor plan. One enters across a porch through a massive Dutch door hung on long black iron hinges. Opening the door reveals the sunny living room, windows wrapping the south and west walls. The old tower's hand-hewn timbers define the room's eight corners, crisscrossing the ceiling. The walls cant inward, a result of the tilting form of the tapered windmill. Spilling from a corner is a wood-paneled stair that climbs the ever-narrowing tower to a conical bedroom, formerly Judge Slicer's study, in the windmill's apex. It is capped in a fan of rough timber supporting the chocolate-pot roof, the walls still in the original salmon plaster.

A wide archway along one side of the living room reveals the dining room, a corner cut by a paneled fireplace decked out in classical dentils, panels, and a swan neck pediment. This seemingly incongruous moment, a remnant from an eighteenth-century house, is a reminder of the shingle style's roots in colonial architecture. Beyond, through a four-panel door, is a modern eat-in kitchen adjoining an open deck raised high above the lawn and the farmland beyond.

Modern features like the deck and kitchen were the result of the owners' skillful renovation. They set about replacing or refurbishing pretty much everything: windows, hardware, plaster, electric, plumbing, air-conditioning, and, of course, the shingles. During the renovation the Dinghy was home. It was subsequently renovated after the completion of Tower House.

Care was taken to protect a defining feature of the house, plaster work by Sydney Burleigh. Architect Edmund Wilson and Burleigh collaborated on the original design. The Slicers were well connected in the political and artistic world of Rhode Island, so it's little surprise that the house combines the efforts of two of the state's prominent designers. At Tower House, Burleigh's decorative flourishes include fleur-de-lis, faux tile patterns, and inspirational slogans. His handprints, side by side with Judge Slicer's, are set into the plaster in an upstairs hall. The design blends the arts and crafts with the shingle style for the original family, who had carved out a lively intellectual life in Little Compton, and the current one, a modern twenty-first-century American family looking for summer sanctuary in Rhode Island.

At the entrance, the 1812 windmill meets the arts and crafts–influenced shingle style interior. The angled timber column leans toward the multi-paneled Dutch door with its wrought hardware.

The former windmill embraced by the 1887 house.

Wind-sculpted trees reach out over the stone wall that lines the road side of the property.

Broad winding treads at the bottom of the staircase spill into the living room.

Burleigh's playful bas-relief plaster tells a story of dueling men-o-war and their flying banners. Stucco masquerading as tilework sits on the low wood wainscot.

HE·TO·HIS·STUDIE·GOES·
AND·THERE·AMIDDES·
SUNDRIE·KINDES·
HE·SEEKES·OUT·MIGHTY·CHARMES·

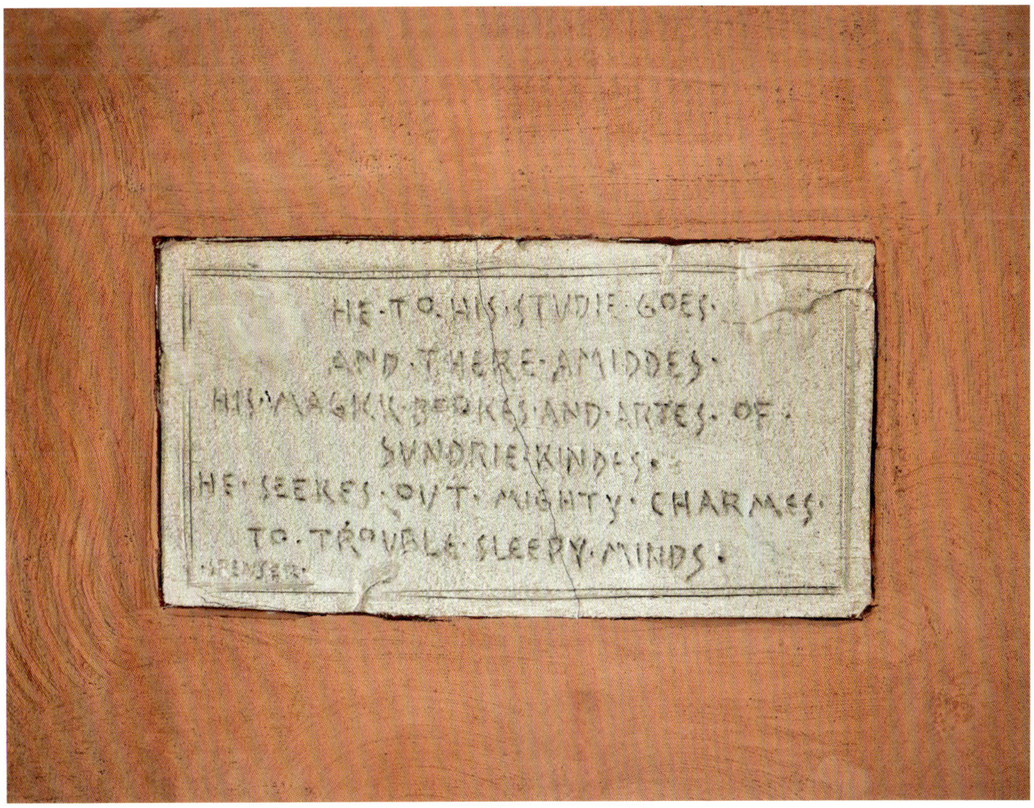

Brilliant persimmon stucco on the drum of the upper bedroom walls. The white plaster dome above the bed suggests a sleeping cap and pleasant dreams.

Handprints purported to be those of owner Slicer and artist accomplice Burleigh. Or are they simply Sidney Burleigh's?

OVERLEAF: The Sakonnet River beyond fence, field, and trees.

Coda

This book opened a giant world for me in this tiny state. At first, assembling sixteen worthy houses seemed nearly impossible, but, as each new acquaintance suggested another, it fell into place. And like delving into any subject, it wasn't long before the multiplying opportunities nearly overwhelmed me. There are more than enough houses for another volume, a challenge I will weigh. Developing agriculture, evolving industries, colonial history, the geography (and geology), wildlife, and architecture combined in a complex web of information. It was an extraordinary undertaking and led to a deeper appreciation for a state that has been part of my entire life.

The houses in the preceding chapters are part of a world we risk losing. Expense, waning interest in historical precedent, and favoring size over simple vernacular are chiming a death knell for these buildings. Many have already been torn down. With climate change, others risk falling into the ocean—the surf is battering at least one I know of into oblivion.

I feel a strong sense of stewardship for the wildlife, nature, and architecture of the Rhode Island coast, and I owe it all a massive debt. All are an important influence on the architecture of Kligerman Architecture & Design, where we strive to imbue our houses with emotion and a deep link to their historical and physical surroundings. We aim to capture the spirit of the work by architects, past and present, famous and unknown, and the bountiful legacy of Rhode Island architecture.

Watercolor of Quonochontaug Pond by the author.

Acknowledgments

I am one of those lone moviegoers, in the dark, reading credits at the end of the film. It takes a long time for the scroll of names to end. There are hundreds of people to acknowledge, and now I understand why. Although this volume is a pipsqueak compared with a feature-length film, there were a ton of hands on deck to make it happen.

The book would never have materialized without the generosity, time, and kindness of homeowners, historians, colleagues, and friends: Daniel Abrashoff, David Andreozzi, Pamela Austen and Tom Risom, The Barrett Family, Valli Budestschu, DeeDee and Jim Buffum, James Buttrick, Donald R. Carlson, Christiane Chidiac, Cristina Del Sesto, Charlotte DuHamel and Greg Licholai, Lisa Dworkin, Louise and Alex Dye, Edith Eglin, John Ferguson, Alicia and Philip Hammarskjold, Kim and Larry Ingeneri, Tori Jones, Duncan Laurie, Keith LeBlanc, Kathyrn and William Low, Peter Manickas, Kari McCabe and Nate McBride, Heidi and Thomas McWilliams, Mary Meade, Jacqui Michel and David Weisman, Deborah Nevins, Suzanne O'Donnell, Mitchell Owens, Rachel and Carl Perry, Miles Redd, Gil Schafer, Robin Squibb, Sally and George Squibb, Courtney Taylor, Nancy Taylor, Christopher Thorpe, John Tschirch, Hans van der Kwast, Charlie Warner, Samuel G. White, and the family of Henry A. Wood III. Each knows his or her contribution.

I am grateful for so many new friendships. All shared their enthusiasm and love of Rhode Island's landscapes, architectural legacy, and history. Owners introduced me to other owners, locals mined their memories for stories that shaped their towns. They are all varied and vital to this work.

At the Westerly Public Library, archivist Nina Wright pulled out boxes of old photographs and folders of yellowed newspaper clippings. Truly a treasure trove.

Sara Frantz has been a driving force and support for so many projects, including this, our third book together. I am grateful for her humor, insight, hard work, and common sense.

This is my fourth book with the Monacelli Press, a division of Phaidon, and editor Elizabeth White. She has given me unparalleled guidance with her deep knowledge of architectural history, always delivered with insight, intelligence, and dry wit. She is a large part of why I waded into another book.

I am grateful to photographer Read McKendree, who knows this state as well as anyone. We palled around on weekends scoping out houses. He introduced me to several of the owners in the book, as well as to many restaurants, tiny lanes, and shortcuts across the state. The photographs were made more beautiful with the help of stylist, furniture lifter, and card Matthew Gleason.

Graphic designer Yolanda Cuomo makes everything beautiful and beautiful things more so. Along with Bobbie Richardson. I can't imagine a more able design duo.

Thank you to my partners at Kligerman Architecture & Design, Joseph Carline, Andrew Davis, Margie Lavender, and Ross Padluck, for their support of this endeavor.

My deepest gratitude is saved for friend, editor, organizer, and champion of my work, Cynthia Conigliaro. Cynthia and I first spoke of writing a book together when studying architecture as college students in Robert A.M. Stern's design studio. Lo and behold, decades later, this is our second volume.

And, as always and ever, Magdalen, Katherine, Rebecca, and Kristin.

First published in 2026

ISBN: 978-1-58093-734-4
Library of Congress Control Number: 2025946189

Photographs by Read McKendree

Except as noted below:
Boston Public Library, Leventhal Collection 18, 70, 184
Block Island Historical Society 10 (bottom left), 11 (bottom)
Cornell University Library 12 (bottom)
William and Kathryn Low (digitization by Greg Anthony) 14
Thomas A. Kligerman 8, 12 (top), 16–17, 32–33, 67–68, 104–5, 122–23, 184–85, 204–5, 234–35, 248–49
Newport Historical Society 10 (bottom right), 13
Private collection 15
Providence Public Library 123, 166
Weekapaug Inn 10 (top right)
Westerly Historical Society 10 (top left), 11 (top)
Yale University, Beinecke Rare Book and Manuscript Library 248

Editor: Elizabeth White
Production: Michael Vagnetti
Design: Yolanda Cuomo and Bobbie Richardson

Printed in China

Phaidon Press Limited
2 Cooperage Yard
London E15 2QR

Monacelli
A Phaidon Company
111 Broadway
New York, NY 10006

Phaidon SARL
55, rue Traversière
75012 Paris

phaidon.com/monacelli